The Rebirth of
England and English
The Vision of William Barnes

Father Andrew Phillips

Anglo-Saxon Books

By the same author

Orthodox Christianity and the Old English Church
The Hallowing of England
Orthodox Christianity and the English Tradition

Published by
Anglo-Saxon Books
www.asbooks.co.uk
in association with
The English Orthodox Trust

Printed and Bound by Lightning Source
Australia, England, USA

Published 1996 ISBN 9781898281177
Reformatted and reprinted 2017

© Fr. Andrew Phillips
© Layout/design Anglo-Saxon Books

ISBN 9781898281733

Jesus answered and said unto him, Verily, verily, I say unto thee, except a man be born again, he cannot see the kingdom of God.

John 3,3

Where there is no vision, the people perish.

Proverbs 29,18

...I hope you will excuse a poor Woman writing to you. I had to dust some Books the other day that came from a sale, and amongst them was your poems in the Dorset dialect. Sir, I shook hands with you in my heart. And I laughed and cried by turns. The old Home of my Youth and all my dear ones mouldering in the earth came back to mind...

My ancestors were Dorset people, and I love the book, it brings back the familiar words of the loved ones that are gone, kindness and affection of your kind and loving heart peeps out at every verse... May you long live to write, and may you long live to read, and may the earth be always blessed with such lights, and may they always be loved and honoured...

Tributes to William Barnes taken from
his daughter's biography of him pp.212–13

Contents

Acknowledgements

I would like to express my sincere thanks to all those who have helped me with this book. First of all to Richard de Peyer, curator of the Dorset County Museum who kindly gave up his time to sift through the Barnes Archive and supply my various needs, including the cover photograph. Secondly to Pearl Linsell who, as usual, has done a wonderful job on the design and typesetting of this book. I also owe a third debt to Fr. Niphon (Carne) of Sturminster Newton, now monk of the Brotherhood of the Orthodox Church of St. Edward the Martyr at Brookwood in Surrey, who has encouraged me in many ways. And last, but hardly least, my heartfelt thanks go out to my wife who gave me that most precious thing, time, to write this work amid the manifold cares of priestly, family and professional life.

Introduction

No city primness trained my feet
To strut in childhood through the street;
But freedom let them loose to tread
The yellow cowslip's downcast head;
Or climb, above the twining hop
And ivy, to the elm-tree's top;
Where southern airs of blue-sky'd day
Breath'd o'er the daisy and the may.
I knew you young, and love you now
O shining grass and shady bough

William Barnes, *Rustic Childhood*

No poet, of the many who are the best glories of England, have we had more true, more sweet, more human and spiritual at once, than this Dorset singer.

Professor Francis Palgrave, 1887

William Barnes (1801–1886) is known as a poet, indeed as the greatest dialect poet of the English language. In the nineteenth century he gained a national literary reputation as 'the Dorset Poet', and was to receive a literary pension from Queen Victoria. He knew many of the literary celebrities of the day such as Tennyson, Allingham, Patmore, Kilvert, Gosse and Hardy who all praised him highly, the latter calling Barnes 'a lyric writer of a high order of genius'. And he has drawn the praise of many: Kingsley, Hopkins, Browning, Forster, Massingham, Auden and Larkin. Sir Arthur Bryant has written that: 'Of all the Victorian writers William Barnes was the humblest and, as time recedes, as we are beginning to realise one of the greatest'.[1] It is not, however, our task here to uncover his literary genius. This has already been done elsewhere and the reader

---

[1] In his Foreword to Hearl, p.xiii

can discover Barnes' poetic genius for himself through the various editions of his poetry in print (See Bibliography).

Certainly we shall often refer to the poetry of William Barnes, but only in the overall context of his life and work. For poetry was only a small part of Barnes' life: 'Poetry was Barnes' love; but philology was his passion'.[2] But even this description of Barnes is far too narrow. For, as we shall see, Barnes was a polymath and a polyglot, familiar with some seventy languages, modern, ancient and oriental, and fluent in fourteen of them; he was interested in everything. This self-taught man from a rural backwater, loving husband and father, priest, poet, teacher extraordinary, writer, linguist of genius, was also draughtsman, engraver, painter, art-collector, mathematician, mechanic, carpenter, gardener, cabinet-maker, clock-maker, political economist, musician, antiquarian, historian, inventor and archaeologist. The present author can only agree with his daughter, Lucy Baxter: 'For one hand to do justice to all the phases of a many-sided mind is not an easy task'.[3]

It is our present goal to look at Barnes as a thinker, remembering that what Barnes thought he also lived. For Barnes was one of those rare people who live by ideas and his way of life matched his thought. This consideration of Barnes as a thinker has never been undertaken before but we feel that it will be of significant and topical importance. It is our belief that we would be mistaken to look at only a part of Barnes' work, for he was above all a man of consistency, he had a wholeness to him that is unknown to those who merely live in the world of headborne booklore. A pupil of Barnes, Rev. O. P. Cambridge said of him: 'His life forms a harmonious whole such as the world rarely sees'.

William Barnes saw through the worldliness of his own times and envisioned the poetic harmony and wholeness of the world as it should have been. 'He saw the indwelling poetry of things'.[4] In plain English,

---

[2] Jacobs, p.5
[3] Baxter, Preface
[4] Jones, Foreword p.6

he saw Eden, he saw Paradise: 'For Barnes, the land of Dorset is close to Eden, and the villager of Dorset close to Adam. Barnes felt that much could be learned about Divine Providence by looking at the natural loveliness of the shire and village life within it'.[5] 'Barnes wanted to preserve the pristine glory of God-created rural England'.[6] 'The Blackmore Vale was a relic of Merry England'.[7] As a deeply religious man Barnes yearned after the Paradise of this other England from before the Fall with all his soul and mind. He sensed the presence of this other 'pre-lapsarian' England and lived in it, either physically in childhood or else spiritually as an adult. He embodied this other England and wished to make known and recreate the wholeness and harmony of it and its speech. This heavenly-minded man wanted this England to be incarnate in historical reality. This was his real life's work, this was his real spiritual vision, or, as he would no doubt have called it, his 'soulsight'.[8]

Barnes then was not just a poet, but a visionary, with an overall view of his country and its language – a view which some would link with Cobbett, Carlyle, Ruskin and Morris. Now a visionary is one who, while seeing the world as it is, also sees the world in an extra dimension – the world as it could be. This is why we have dared to call this modest work, 'The Rebirth of England and English', for that, we believe, is what Rev. William Barnes, in his own discreet, unassuming but visionary way, was seeking, working and praying for – his vision was that of an England and English reborn. As the Encyclopaedia Britannica says of him: 'His poetry is essentially English in character, no other writer has given quite so simple and sincere a picture of the homely life and labour of rural England'. And his Bishop (the nephew of Wordsworth, whom with Burns Barnes recognised as a master) wrote of him that, 'what most struck myself, was his serene and guileless character, and his sympathy with the best

---

[5] Keane, p.14
[6] Forsyth, p.152
[7] Ruffell, p.8
[8] Baxter, p.286

side of English country life'.[9] And a later writer has said: 'Although there are few overt patriotic expressions of it, Barnes' love for England is present in almost every line he wrote.'[10] This is why in this work we shall speak of his 'vision' in the many areas which interested him.

The word 'vision' may seem alien to our often cruelly pragmatic age but is not society the poorer for having no vision to strive towards? Though we know that a vision may be unattainable, a society without vision is directionless, disorientated and, having lost its bearings, drifts towards unknown and dangerous destinations. The human soul cannot live without vision. The Victorian Age, for example, believed in the pragmatism of Progress. Barnes opposed that Progress,[11] seeing through its guileful and soul-destroying reality with his vision: 'Barnes' achievement is enhanced in that it stands in direct opposition to the idea of Progress'.[12] What followed Progress, two World Wars and a planet ever hovering on the brink of some new catastrophe, nuclear or ecological, would seem to confirm that Barnes may have been right all along and today we are in a position to sympathise more with Barnes' vision than the now dethroned idea of Progress of the Victorian Age. 'To an age which has seen so many and such great changes, the poems of Barnes are a glimpse into the heart of one aspect of Christendom as it has grown up through centuries'.[13] And it is our belief, expressed in the following pages, that our post-industrial society, in search of authentic English roots and values may well have much to learn from Barnes' surprisingly relevant pre-industrial values and ideals.

---

[9] Baxter, p.321

[10] Levy, p.18

[11] Following the publication of Mill's essay in 1861, Barnes actually wrote a refutation of Utilitarianism. Barnes totally disagreed with Mill, saying that he had looked at man only as a physical being, overlooking his mind and soul (Baxter, pp. 224–5)

[12] Forsyth, p.138

[13] Bernard Jones, *The Poems*, Vol. I, p.21

Part One

The Rebirth of England

Chapter 1

The Life of William Barnes

Seek ye first the kingdom of God, and his righteousness.

Matt. 6,33

William Barnes was born on 22 February 1801 in the beautiful Dorset countryside of the Blackmore Vale at Rush-Hay, a smallholding at Bagber Common near Sturminster Newton. His father, John, was a poor smallholder. His mother, Grace, who died when William was five, came from the neighbouring village of Fifehead Neville. Though William was the fifth of six children, his mother still had time to instil in him a love of beauty, music, art and poetry which he was never to forget. Barnes recalled his adored mother in poems, 'Mother O' Mothers', 'Fifehead' and 'The Mornen Moon', where he wrote: 'An' she that there, so good an' kind, Awoke to thought my childhood's mind'. His daughter, Lucy, wrote that 'the minds of great men are influenced by their mothers'.[14] The Barnes had lived in the Vale since the sixteenth century (originating from Barnes in Surrey) and the Vale was where William felt deeply his roots. After losing his mother, Barnes, a shy and delicate child, together with his brothers and sisters went to live at their aunt's and uncle's farm at nearby Pentridge Farm, also in the Vale.

In spite of losing his mother, Barnes' childhood was blissful and he was marked deeply by it for the rest of his life, constantly recalling it in his poetry. It should be remembered that all this was before both the Enclosures and the Industrial Revolution and railways reached Dorset. In a sense Barnes was to spend the rest of his life striving to recapture the lost Paradise of the England and the English speech that he had known and loved so well in his childhood. His poetry is redolent of nostalgia for the sweet innocence of country life and he

---

[14] Baxter, p.8

was to return on pilgrimage to this childhood many times throughout his adult life. Indeed by 1847, after his father's death the previous year, he had saved enough to buy two fields at Bagber, which was his way of re-attaching himself to his roots as to an umbilical cord. Of this event he wrote, 'The Pleace Our Own Again' and 'I Got Two Vields'. In verse after verse that he wrote he was always to compare the country favourably with the town. Thus in possibly his most famous poem, later set to music by Vaughan-Williams, the mellifluous 'My Orcha'd in Linden Lea', he wrote in a slightly adapted Dorset dialect:

> Let other vo'k [folk] meake money vaster
> In the air o' dark-room'd towns,
> I don't dread a peevish master;
> Though noo man do heed my frowns,
> I be free to goo abrode [abroad],
> Or take agean my hwomeward road
> To where, vor me, the apple tree
> Do lean down low in Linden Lea.

[Throughout this book, wherever dialect words in poems may present difficulties, the author has placed an English translation in brackets after them]. In many other poems such as 'Praise O' Do'set', 'Childhood', 'Pentridge by the River', 'Uncle an' Aunt', 'Blackmwore Maidens', 'Our Be'thplace', 'Be'mi'ster', 'Our Fathers' Works', 'Woodley', 'The Woodland Home', William Barnes records with heartfelt nostalgia this childhood bliss. And in some of his most popular comic pieces, 'John Bloom in Lon'on' and 'Sam'el Down Vrom Lon'on', he gently mocks the townee, compared unfavourably with the 'landfolk' of Dorset. Let us quote just one more poem recording his childhood:

> Wi' [With] buoyish heart I vound [found]
> The twitterin' birds a builded round
> Your high-boughed hedges, zunny woodlands.
> You gi'ed [gave] me life, you gi'ed me jay [joy],
> Lwonesome woodlands, zunny woodlands,

You gi'ed me health, as in my play
I rambled through ye, zunny woodlands.

It was this childhood which aroused Barnes' curiosity, giving rise later to his interest in language, folklore and antiquities. Barnes made things with his hands, sketched, read and wrote poetry, recalled in a comic poem 'The Young Rhymer Snubbed'. School was in Sturminster Newton and here Barnes soon demonstrated his phenomenal intelligence. Aged thirteen, he left school, having easily found work as a solicitor's clerk in Sturminster, thanks to his general intelligence and beautiful handwriting.

At this time, after the end of the French War at Waterloo in 1815, agriculture had fallen into depression and Barnes' uncle, like so many others, was bankrupted. Such sad events he would later record in poems. Barnes left the Vale in 1818 to live in Dorchester, working as a clerk, much as he had done in Sturminster. Here, with the encouragement of local clergy, his genius flourished and he began to teach himself foreign languages and became more interested in music, archaeology and antiquarianism. It was also in the same year that he saw a sixteen year-old girl from Saffron Walden in Essex, Julia Miles, the daughter of a newly-arrived excise-officer. He fell in love with her at first sight and wished to marry her. But given her and Barnes' youth and his modest position, marriage was out of the question for the time being. His love for Julia was to inspire Barnes to publish poetry and his 'Poetical Pieces' were actually printed in Dorchester in 1820. Here Barnes pursued his other interests too, including copper and wood engraving and considered becoming an engraver. In 1822 he and Julia were betrothed, but this did not solve his financial problems. The solution came the following year when, with Julia's encouragement this self-taught, self-made man became a schoolmaster.

Thus it was that in 1823 Barnes went to Mere, just over the Dorset border in Wiltshire, to take up the position of schoolmaster, imparting wisdom to his charges and bettering himself in the eyes of his future father-in-law. Barnes was to spend four years here as a solitary and impoverished schoolmaster, writing love-letters to Julia, constantly improving himself, studying and learning new languages: French,

Latin, Greek, Russian, Persian, German, Italian. Moreover he read in these languages, often poetry (he loved and translated Petrarch), and was later to use the techniques of the poetry of these languages in his own poetry. The experience that he gained in teaching was to provide him with an income that would last for nearly forty years. This period may be called his apprenticeship, which ended on 9 July 1827 with his marriage to Julia.

Then began an idyllic period of domesticity. The bliss of married life was to produce seven children: Laura Liebe (named after Petrarch's Laura) was born in 1829 (died 1918), Julia Eliza in 1832 (d. 1915), Julius in 1834 (d. 1837), Lucy Emily in 1837 (d. 1902), Isabel in 1838 (d. 1906), William Miles in 1840 (d. 1916) and Egbert in 1843 (d. 1877). (By 1882 there were seventeen grandchildren; one great grandchild is still alive). All these children, apart from Julius, survived into adulthood and had successful careers. Julia herself was the ideal spouse for this unworldly genius, her schoolmaster husband, who at this period had begun to dress somewhat eccentrically in a blue dressing-gown, a trait that was to last the rest of his life. Not only was Julia beautiful but she was also full of practical common sense and organisation. As for Barnes, a brilliant, humorous and most original pedagogue, teaching a huge range of subjects in a school with both day-pupils and now boarders, he also continued to cultivate himself, learning new languages, including Welsh (which he practised on holiday in Wales) and Hindustani, and making use of his considerable artistic and scientific talents. This homely man made furniture, gardened, played the organ, piano, flute and violin, wrote plays, engraved, made scientific instruments and began publishing articles on government, etymology, philology, local history and mathematics. He often wrote letters and articles for journals and the local *Dorset County Chronicle* where his first dialect poems were published. These included his 'Eclogues' with their discreetly disguised social criticism of the conditions of the rural poor – the case of the Tolpuddle Martyrs had arisen in 1834. This Wiltshire period was to end in 1835 when he moved back to Dorchester where Julia saw much better prospects.

Here he set up another school, which was academically and, thanks to Julia, financially, successful. In Dorchester, where the Barnes family with the expanding school was to move three times to new premises, Barnes continued publishing articles on widely diverse topics as well as writing school primers especially on Science and Language. In addition he continued to write in the local newspaper. In all, Barnes was eventually to write 34 books or essays as well as dozens of shorter articles and reviews in magazines and newspapers, totalling some 95 pieces of work. Many of them were written at this time, many were on philology and antiquarianism, others were school-books on an extraordinarily wide range of subjects. At the same time, as a devout layman, he was visiting and helping the poor. In 1837, following the sad death of his three year-old son Julius, Barnes took up a course of study at the University of Cambridge that would result in his being ordained an Anglican clergyman in 1847 and receiving a Bachelor of Divinity degree in 1850, having by then spent three full terms at the University – to the detriment of his school and at the cost of the self-sacrifice of his family. However, the greatest public event of this period was in 1844 when he published *Poems of Rural Life in the Dorset Dialect*, complete with a dissertation and glossary of the Dorset dialect. This was to be the first of his volumes of dialect poetry, which were all to be reprinted several times both during his lifetime and after it, and would establish him first as a County then a National figure. Significantly this first volume of dialect poetry also included a defence of the Dorset dialect, in which he recognised the linguistic heritage of the West Saxon of King Alfred, the literary language of Saxon England. Barnes' intention in his poetry was in no way to mock the speech and customs of what Victorian Society called 'rustics', on the contrary he wrote as one of them and in defence of them, with love and sympathy for them. Nevertheless in 1846 he was persuaded by a patroness, the poetess Caroline Norton, to write another volume of poetry in 'National' or 'London' English, but the quality of most of the poetry in it was markedly lower. Significantly, again in this linguistic connection, in 1849 Barnes wrote a primer of Anglo-Saxon, for use in classroom – a pioneering work in the field.

In 1851 William Barnes, poet, schoolmaster and curate of the tiny hamlet of Whitcombe, three miles outside Dorchester, seemed to be at the height of his powers. But this was not really the case. Probably on account of his championing of the Dorset dialect, his original (and very effective – Barnes never used corporal punishment at a time when flogging was usual) teaching methods, the fact that he himself had had no education, being only a peasant-farmer's son, and also no doubt on account of his eccentric dress, he was rejected by the local Establishment, who in 1847 had refused to appoint him headmaster of the local Grammar School – a bitter disappointment for Barnes. It was in 1847 that he had written a collection of articles called 'Humilis Domus' ('The Humble Home'), and here he ventured into the territory of political economy. Again he expressed his sympathy for the plight of the rural poor, though he was clearly opposed to any kind of revolt or organised opposition of farm-workers to the exploitation of the times.

Barnes' happiness was to be shattered in 1852 when Julia fell ill with breast cancer. All too quickly on 21 June Barnes' beloved Julia died. The suddenness of her death left Barnes greatly distraught. After 25 years of married bliss it was an event from which neither he nor his school would ever recover. He was devastated and aged ten years in a matter of months. Only later would his grief be expressed in some of his most moving poetry, 'Plorata Veris Lachrymis', 'The Wife A'Lost', 'My Dearest Julia' and 'Woak [Oak] Hill', 'The Leady's Tower', 'The Wold Wall', 'The Trial Past'. In the first of these he wrote:

> How can I live my lonesome days?
> How can I tread my lonesome ways?
> How can I take my lonesome meal?
> Or how outlive the grief I feel?

In 1853 his mother-in-law who had helped at the school also died and in 1854 Barnes himself was for a time critically ill. He began, probably unconsciously, to neglect the school, which his two eldest daughters, Laura and Julia, were now running. It became clear that the financial success of the school had depended very largely on the frugality and great efficiency of Julia. Barnes more and more took refuge in his Faith, his learning and his writings, especially writings concerning the revival of Old English which contains the Saxon roots of Modern English.

In 1854 he published *A Philological Grammar*, which showed his amazing knowledge of some seventy languages from all over the world. His idea was that if one could understand the structures of language, then one could learn to master any language; he himself took only one to two weeks to learn how to read a language with the aid of a dictionary. Noticeably, some of the vocabulary he used in *A Philological Grammar* was not Standard English but Barnes' own invented 'Saxon' English, which avoided words of Latin or French origin. Although he had begun inventing new words on the basis of Old English roots long before, this was the first time he had used it in a living way to express himself.

At the same time Barnes continued his unpaid, voluntary work as a secretary of the Dorset County Museum that he had helped to set up some ten years before, with working-men's associations (Mechanics' Institutes), where he lectured and gave highly popular poetry readings, and with visiting the sick and the poor. It was becoming more and more apparent that Barnes' deepest vocation was not really that of a teacher. In 1858 a new volume of nostalgic poems, *Hwomely Rhymes* appeared, and in the following year he wrote, again in a Saxonising English, *Views of Labour and Gold*, where Barnes wrote of political economy. In the same year, 1859, Barnes translated the Song of Solomon into the Dorset dialect at the behest of none other than Prince Lucien Bonaparte, the distinguished French linguist who visited Barnes twice. In 1861, the year in which he received a modest Literary Pension, he wrote *TIW; or, a View of the Roots and Stems of English as a Teutonic Tongue*, another highly original linguistic work.

In the meantime, the school in Dorchester had declined disastrously and in 1862 it was closed, virtually bankrupt. It should be mentioned that his poetry and other writings brought Barnes virtually no income. Just in time, Barnes was offered the living of Winterborne Came, one mile outside Dorchester. After thirty nine years as a schoolmaster Barnes was going to become a country rector on a stipend of £200 per annum. He had been saved from poverty and homelessness, not by his teaching, but by the Church: he was justified by his faith

Barnes went to live in the charming thatched rectory (which still stands with little change) with five of his children and also grandchildren – and nearly fifty yards of bookshelves. He took up his position with his usual integrity, piety and kindness to the poor. His daughter relates how one parishioner said of Barnes, 'There, miss, we do all o' us love the passon [parson], that we do: he be so plain'.[15] From now on he was to divide most of his time between care for the souls entrusted to him, his charitable work in lecturing and reading all over the South-West for working men's associations, and his intellectual and poetic preoccupations. These were combined in the brilliant but unofficial work he did on notes for a revised translation of the Bible and his translation of Psalms from a comparison of the Hebrew and the Septuagint. Of this period his daughter wrote how Barnes would sit in the Edenic garden that he had created around the thatched rectory: 'In this floral nook the poet would place his basket-work seat, and with his eyes closed and face upturned into the sunlight, he would sit for an hour at a time, sometimes brooding poetry through the medium of visions, sometimes thinking out a deep question of ethics or philosophy...'.[16] In the same way Barnes would also often walk to the nearby ruin of a fourteenth century church at Winterborne Farringdon, and there he would sit and pray. 'In other churches I teach – here I come to learn', he said.[17]

In 1862 a third and final collection of dialect poems was published, followed in 1868 by more 'National English' poems. His poetry was then to be reprinted many times in the coming years and after his death into the present century. In 1863 *A Grammar and Glossary of the Dorset Dialect* came out. Thus, despite his very time-consuming pastoral work as a priest which he carried out with great

---

[15] op. cit., p.201
[16] op. cit., p.247
[17] Baxter, p.208

conscientiousness and sincerity, walking up to twenty miles a day visiting his parishioners, as well as his literary work, William Barnes managed to continue his antiquarian and linguistic activities. In particular in 1869 he wrote *Early England and the Saxon-English* and in 1878 *An Outline of English Speech-Craft* (An English Grammar) and in 1880 *An Outline of Rede-Craft* (Logic), these last three quite extraordinary books written largely in his own Saxon English, full of neologisms based on Old English speech.

As we come to the end of Barnes' life, we see a long-haired, white-bearded, softly-spoken man, an eccentric or crank to the Establishment but a priest-poet loved by his parishioners and adored by children and his own grandchildren. He would receive visits from famous literary men, linguists and also the curious from America. Thus in 1881 Arthur Quiller-Couch, later Professor of English Literature at Cambridge: 'The house straw-thatched – rioted over by creepers – was set around with trees. Swallows populated its eaves; bees hummed in its garden. I am painting you (however you suspect it) no nook of fancy, but the residence of an actual man, whom you will find at once idyllic, shrewd and solid. He is just past eighty, but hale yet, white bearded with an aspect which suggests what you can recollect of Saint Mark from any number of stained glass windows. His hair, too, is white and he wears it patriarchally long so that it touches his shoulders. He is dressed in a long black coat, knee-breeches, black stockings, stout buckled shoes…'.[18] The diarist Kilvert wrote: 'I was immediately struck by the beauty and grandeur of his head. It was an apostolic head, bald and venerable, and the long, soft silvery hair flowed on his shoulders and a long white beard fell on his breast… He is a very remarkable and remarkable-looking man, half hermit, half enchanter'.[19] And a contemporary biographer writes: 'He had become revered and respected, a sage and polymath, living out his life in a paradise lapped still by the sea of faith'.[20] Another visitor described how the day would start with morning

---

[18] Sir Arthur Quiller-Couch, *The Poet as Citizen*, CUP, 1934, pp.174–196
[19] Dugdale, p.202
[20] Chedzoy, Foreword to *Poems Grave and Gay*, p.viii

prayers and how he 'spoke in pure English, with a beautiful simplicity and correctness'.[21] In 1884, as Barnes was walking home with his neighbour Thomas Hardy, whom Barnes influenced considerably, a sudden rainstorm broke out. Rev. William Barnes caught cold and from then on for the next two years he surely but steadily declined.

For much of these two years Barnes was bed-ridden and unable to venture out. His daughters grieved about this, but Barnes reassured them: 'It does not matter much to me for I have my inward sight... I am never less alone than when alone – I have my own thoughts... All kinds of thoughts – the welfare and happiness of mankind – the forms of language and of speech...'.[22] On the night of 5 October 1886 Barnes woke up from a dream and said to his daughter: 'I have seen that pretty sheltered nook again. The sea runs into a little cove there, it is my little place I know it. There was a steamer gliding in the waves and the stream all glistens in the sun – there are hills all around the place, belted with woods, down to the water's edge'.[23] It was the countryman's exotic dream of Paradise, the dream of the sea. During the following night, that of the 6 October, he awoke from sleep and prayed with his daughter Laura, 'Lighten our darkness we beseech Thee, O Lord'. The following morning, 7 October, he composed some couplets, the last of which was: 'Dry our eyes in weeping, Shut our eyes in sleeping'. Then he was heard to say: 'I want to say that I am thankful for all – for this sickness – for the pain – I am thankful'. Laura went to the parlour and slept a little. When she awoke she found her father dead. He had died peacefully in his sleep: 'He fell into a sweet slumber and no-one knew the moment when he stepped over the boundary into the invisible world and dreamed his way into Paradise'.[24]

He was buried in the little graveyard of Winterborne Came on 11 October 1886, his grave marked with a Celtic cross. His son,

---

[21] Baxter, p.286
[22] Hinchy, p.63
[23] op. cit. above
[24] Baxter, p.326

William Miles Barnes, who had followed his father into the Anglican priesthood, wrote to their diocesan Bishop of Salisbury, Christopher Wordsworth: 'For the last few days he had dreams in his sleep and waking visions of scenes which were beautiful and which he described. He had not dreamed in his life before and as he had a poet's love for all things bright and beautiful, these were a great pleasure to him... He was a man most gentle in disposition, but of great passive courage, of pure life and simple faith'.[25] In February 1887 the same bishop, who had known Barnes personally, unveiled a statue of William Barnes, which still stands today in the centre of Dorchester, symbolically outside the main St. Peter's Church, next to the Dorset County Museum. On it a plaque, quoting from Barnes' own poetry, reads:

> Zoo [So] now I hope his kindly feäce
> Is gone to find a better pleäce;
> But still, wi' vo'k [with folk] a-left behind
> He'll always be a-kept in mind.

What were the views and visions, the world-outlook of the 'greatest man Dorset has produced',[26] this extraordinary poet-priest, 'of pure life and simple faith'?

---

[25] Hinchy, pp.65–6
[26] Hearl, p.190

Chapter 2

Religion

There is no happiness without knowledge of God.

Abbot Aelfric, Sermon on the Nativity of the Lord,
written at Cerne Abbey, Dorset c.996

'God is love', and His word is our guide to happiness – not to misery.

William Barnes, Sermon on the Day of Humiliation, 1857

A child of God is a child of glory.

Sermon at Whitcombe, 9 October 1881

At church with meek and unaffected grace,
His looks adorn'd the venerable place;
Truth from his lips prevail'd with double sway,
And fools who came to scoff, remain'd to pray.

Oliver Goldsmith, *The Deserted Village*, 1770

William Barnes was an orthodox churchman and clergyman of the Anglican Church. Of the need of man to be a member of the Church he wrote: 'A ship cannot steer itself aright from within – the rudder must be without that steers a ship. Neither can a compass be of use unless the Pole from without attracts it. The Soul requires a fixed standard of excellence without itself to attain to'.[27] At first it would seem that though he might dress strangely, Barnes was very much a conformist. But in 1839 this layman of the Established Church, who neither drank nor smoked, who was a church organist and voluntary district visitor, was also translating Hindu religious texts. He was far from being an average Victorian churchman. Many of the values that he held were so traditional that in the context of Victorian churchmanship he was a radical – in other words he was too spiritually-minded to be a conformist, his heart was too alive to the

---

[27] Quoted Dugdale, p.196

needs of the world and his fellow-man to blindly follow the fashions of the day. Indeed this is the sense of his unusual dress.

It has been said that William Barnes was neither a religious poet nor a mystic. Although some poems certainly touched on religious themes (e.g. 'Vo'k A-Comen Into Church – 'Praÿr a-bringen welcome rest so softly to the troubled breast') and he did write some fifteen 'hymns', six 'Sabbath Lays' and a religious drama 'Ruth', we could agree with this judgement. But in another sense all his poetry, like his whole life and all his works, was deeply religious, for his religion was so natural that it was completely unconscious: 'His poetry never attempts the impassioned re-enactment of Christian experience... Barnes is a religious poet only in the sense that his writing is replete with a sense of the holiness of all things'.[28] As our poet put it in his poem 'The Railroad':

> Zoo [So] while our life do last, mid [might] nought
> But what is good an' feäir be sought,
> In word or deed, or heart or thought,
> An' all the rest wheel round it.

Barnes would never have thought of himself as 'mystical' or 'religious', in the same way that a saint would never think of himself as 'mystical' or 'religious'. Such thoughts are the province of the pretentious and self-deluded. As Blessed Augustine wrote in the fifth century: 'The human soul is naturally Christian'. For Barnes it was a deformation of nature not to be a Christian. Writing in an article on Christian Marriage, he said: 'All that is against God is against our happiness'[29] – and as Barnes might have added – who wishes to be unhappy? Only Barnes could have written in a book on Economics that 'the true happiness of man is holiness'.[30]

Like his poetry, the inspiration for his religion simply came to him. 'He is of no school but that of nature', wrote the poet Coventry Patmore, whom Barnes admired. 'I doubt if Barnes ever quite looked

---

[28] Chedzoy, Afterword to *Poems Grave and Gay*, p.xvi
[29] *The Ladies' Treasury* 1 April 1866, p.197
[30] *Views of Labour and Gold*, p.120

upon himself as a 'poet' in our conscious European way'.[31] Barnes invented the word 'Faith-law' to translate the Latin word religion into his 'Saxonised' English. In other words, according to Barnes, if one had faith, the laws by which to live naturally followed from it. This is why Barnes spoke so little of the great dispute of the Victorian Age, that between Science and Religion, crystallised in the controversy around Darwinism. Barnes could not understand how anybody could possibly doubt that man had been created by God:

> Tis happiness to know
> That there's a God above us;
> An' He, by day an' night, do ho [care]
> Vor all ov us, an' love us.

So he wrote in 'The Bells Ov Alderburnham'.

For him Faith was so obvious, that he was unable to enter into debate. As he wrote in his book, *Rede-Craft*: 'There is a vast deal [amount] of wrangling [argument] which is idle [vain] for the finding of truth, and kindles anger for want of clear definitions which cannot be sought too carefully; for when one man upholds against another a so-taken [hypothetical] truth under a name by which the other understands something else, their reasonings do not run on the same line, and cannot reach the same upshot [conclusion]. There are things of great weight in the world, and yet, while their names are very rife [common] in speech and writing, it is not easy to formark [define] them, and I am sometimes ready to say that I do not understand the meaning of a single word'.[32] [Throughout this book words in prose texts in brackets explain Barnes' 'Saxon' English words which may present the reader with difficulty]. 'It seems to us that we should always keep asunder [separate] outward world-truth [factual truth], which is rightly the end of inductive reason, and inward soul-truth [spiritual truth], which is the end of faith; and that if we set inductive reasoning to work in the dominion of faith, soul-truth, we may become unbelievers; and if we send out faith, in the place of reason,

---

[31] Grigson, p.6
[32] *Rede-Craft*, p.45

to seek world-truth, we may be superstitious'.[33] And again in a sermon he said that 'knowledge is merely a tool, wisdom a skill'.[34] Man was to seek wisdom by knowledge. In his poem 'The Happy Days When I Wer Young' he also referred to his bewilderment:

Vrom where wer all this venom brought
To kill our hope an' taint our thought?
Clear brook! Thy water coulden bring
Sich [Such] venom vrom thy rocky spring.

The venom referred to was 'what's a-talked about by many now – that to despise The laws o' God an' man is wise'.

Perhaps the most outstanding aspect of this unselfconscious spirituality of Barnes is his profound belief in the presence of God all around him. In his poem 'Tweil' [Toil] Barnes wrote: 'Zoo [So] I woon't live in fear o' men, But man-neglected, God-directed, Still wull tweil an' tweil ageän'. These words in many ways sum up the whole of Barnes' often very hard life. Especially when his beloved Julia died and he faced financial hardship and even ruin, he was borne by his faith, and at moments by nothing but his faith. At heart an orthodox Christian, aware of the presence of God all around him, he suffered in the world. He believed in what he called 'the higher law of righteousness in the Gospel'. He looked through the world around him 'to see the inner meaning of things', as his daughter wrote of him,[35] to see in other words the providential actions of the God of Love at work in the world of men. He had the perspicacity, the ability to see through the shallow bourgeois Victorian values of 'tradesmanship' [commercialism] which was all around him and into the Saxon mind and soul and speech of 'folk' England. This was to see the essence of things as they really are, to see the divine origin of all things, the original harmony of Creation, that which Darwin could never see.

---

[33] Quoted in Grigson, pp.35-6
[34] Sermon on 27th August 1876 in Came
[35] Baxter, p.44

This belief, as we shall see, deeply affected Barnes' understanding of aesthetics, the beautiful in Nature and Art. Since he saw God in all things, he was interested in all things, he was a polymath, having universal culture. Thus Science too was but a proof of God's existence: 'The task of the scientist, considered Barnes, was to reveal God's laws in the material world, as he himself had sought such laws in Science, Art, Language, Social Economics and Education'.[36] 'This is also why he was a poet (in Greek, poet means 'creator'), for he recreated what he saw in the work of the Creator. And this is why he took the most radical step of all, by becoming a priest, becoming 'a representative of the only institution which he felt (at that time) had the power to save the nation's soul from materialism, and bridge the ever-widening gulf, as he then saw it, between rich and poor, employer and employed, landed and landless'.[37]

This perspicacity, the ability to sense God's Presence around him, is reflected in his profound belief in Providence and his acceptance of God's Will, which is reflected in so very many of his poems. In his poem 'Woone [One] Rule', he gave utterance to the profound but pithy and simple conclusion that he had reached about life: '

> What is, is best, We needen fear,
> An' we shall steer to happy rest.

and

> Our God ha' gi'ed us, vrom our youth,
> Woone rule to be our guide – His Truth.

In another poem, 'Things Do Come Round', he wrote:

> O thread o' love by God unwound,
> How He in time do bring things round.

---

[36] Hearl, p.299
[37] op. cit. p.224

And in his 'Good Measter Collins':

> ...what God do zend [send]
> Is best vor [for] all o's [of us] in the end,
> An' all that we do need the mwost
> Do come to us wi' leäst o' cost...
> Zoo let us never pine in sin,
> Vor gifts that ben't [aren't] the best to win;
> The heaps o' goold that zome mid pile,
> Wi' sleepless nights an' peaceless tweil;

And in another poem, 'Vields by Watervalls', he said:

> We mid [might] have noo e'thly love;
> But God's love-tokens vrom above
> Here mid greet us, In the vields by watervalls'.

Barnes had a childlike faith in Providence, which he reiterated in so many poems such as 'Happy Times', 'Zickness', 'Grammer A-Crippled' or 'Body An' Mind':

> All vrom Providence above,
> Must ever show,
> To souls below,
> That God is wisdom, and is love.

In an Eclogue, 'The New Poor Laws', he expressed this faith thus: '

> My trust a bin in GOD, an' not in man,
> Var [For] HE've a promised us to gi'e
> Whate'er is good for us; an' HE can zee;
> Var all the wordle da belong to HE.

Thus in his 'Humilis Domus' he wrote against the hopeless fatalism of Malthusianism: 'Are we not sinful in blaming the land, or the increase of human life, and through it, God, for social evils which should never be imputed to Him, inasmuch as He does not make such great blunders in the economy of the world, as those to which we are pleased to conceive we can refer evil consequences'.[38] For Barnes,

---

[38] *Poole and Dorset Herald*, 17 May 1849

Creation was ordered by the Higher Wisdom of the Maker in harmony and orderliness. In his poem 'Two-an-Two', he wrote:

> By two an' two,
> How goodly things do goo,
> A-matchen woone another to fulvill
> The goodness ov their Maker's will.
> By peäir an' peäir
> Each thing's a meäde to sheäre
> The good another can bestow,
> In wisdom's work down here below.

Barnes' faith in Providence also comes out in the poems that he wrote after Julia's death: 'By storms a-toss'd, I'll gi'e God praïse, Wi' much a-lost I still ha' jaÿs.' ('Blessens A-Left'), 'Hast thou rememberèd my servant Job?' ('The Leady's Tower'), 'An' yet, while things do come an' goo, God's love is steadfast, John, an' true.' ('Rivers Don't Gi'e Out'), and in 'The Weather-Beaten Tree':

> But He will never meäke our sheäre
> O' sorrow mwore than we can bear,
> But meäke us zee, if 'tis His will,
> That He can bring us good vrom ill.

Or again in 'The Trial Past':

> How melting is the backward thought
> That 'twas His love alone that wrought
> What I had deem'd His anger brought.
> So blest is he that can abide
> His day of sorrowing when tried,
> Enduring to the end.

Perhaps his very orthodox conclusion is best expressed in 'The Thorns in the Geate':

> An' zoo in life let us vulvil
> Whatever is our Meäker's will,
> An' then bide still, wi' peacevul breast,
> While He do manage all the rest.

And in his poem 'Happiness' he wrote: 'If there is rest 'ithin the breast, 'Tis where the heart is holy.' And in another poem, 'Thatchen O' The Rick', he had written: 'Contentment is a constant feäst, He's richest that do want the leäst.'

In several now rather Victorian poems concerning the death of children and their grieving parents, for example 'Sleep Did Come Wi' The Dew', 'Meary-Ann's Child', 'A Life', 'The Mother's Dream' (we should not forget the death of Barnes' three-year old son, Julius), Barnes also expressed his faith in the after-life, and souls 'to heaven a-vled'. This theme of the loving Providence of God is also expressed in the prayers that he composed: 'O Lord of Wisdom and Love give me in affliction faith in Thy providence and mercy. Let me but feel and know that my afflictions come from Thee and they will seem light'....' No sorrow has affrighted us, Sickness has not kept us waking and trials of Sorrow have not broken our peace. May we be mindful of Thy full and abundant goodness and become more and more convinced that Thy Service is perfect freedom and that Thy yoke is easy and though in fatherly connection Thou mayst put upon us trials of timely and wholesome afflictions yet, that supported by Thy Holy Spirit we shall find Thy burdens light'.[39] Finally we would like to quote from one of the hymns that he wrote, 'Teach us how to pray':

> O Lord we pray not as we ought
> We pray in word but not in thought
> Our hearts are dull and cold: we kneel
> And tell of wants we do not feel
> But warm our chilly hearts of clay
> And teach us teach us how to pray.
> We ask for power, we ask for gold
> We ask what mercy must withhold
> We ask for life and earthly bliss
> And fail because we ask amiss

---

[39] Hinchy, pp.63-64

But take our blindness, Lord, away
And teach us teach us how to pray.[40]

In all things William Barnes was humble and meek, loving God's creation. He was a model, self-sacrificing and loving pastor – as the ten boxes of manuscript sermons in the Dorset County Museum Barnes Collection witness. He loved his family, loved children and the poor. He was kind to animals at a time when kindness to animals was not especially encouraged, he had 'a true and loving heart' (Rev. O. P. Cambridge). He believed in doing good (his poem 'Do Good': 'So give with kindly hands, For God can give you more') and wrote: 'Zoo while our life do last, mid nought But what is good an' feäir be sought' ('The Railroad II'). He had great compassion: 'Heavy do vall, Trials on all The jaÿ-seeken hearts ov poor stricken mankind' ('Body An' Mind'), and, 'Vor they that can but mercy show Shall all their Father's mercy win' ('Pity'). In all living beings he saw the inner harmony of Creation, the Unseen Hand of the Maker, a pattern of love arranging all by colour and shape. He sought and found harmony in all things, Nature, Art and Science, because he naturally saw all things through the eyes of faith. If his beloved Julia was 'the creative mainspring' of his life, then deep religious faith was undoubtedly the mainstay of his life, and it is this that we shall see again and again in the coming chapters as we investigate his views on Nature and Art, Marriage, Society, Economics, Politics and his beliefs con-cerning the English Language. Natural, unselfconscious, unpretentious, simple but most deep religious faith is the key which unlocks all the doors in Barnes' life and thought. Thinking of Barnes' faith, we are reminded of Tennyson's famous lines:

Kind hearts are more than coronets,
And simple faith more than Norman blood.

---

[40] Ms. Hymn in the Barnes Collection in the Dorset County Museum

Chapter 3

Nature and Art

The aim of high art is the seeing and interpreting of God's Will
and a working with His Truth.

William Barnes, *Thoughts on Beauty and Art*, p.132

If society owes a debt to those poets and artists who make a
nation conscious of its better self, and set before it, as true
ministers of God, the ideal of excellence which is within its grasp
as part of His Creation, surely this is true of our Dorset poet.

Bishop Christopher Wordsworth, Baxter, p.322

'There is no art without love. Every artist who has produced anything
worthy has had a love of his subject. The old artists, as Raphael and
his school, had a true love of religion, and therefore painted true
works of Art in a religious spirit'.[41] So spoke Rev. William Barnes.
And these were not empty words, for he lived by them. 'Love' was a
word which ran like a refrain through his poems. 'If the key-word to
his life is 'industry', that to his poems is love'.[42] Thus in his
'dissertation' or introduction to his first volume of dialect poetry in
1844 he wrote: 'The author thinks his readers will find his Poems free
of slang and vice, as they are written from the associations of an early
youth that was passed among rural families in a secluded part of the
county, upon whose sound Christian principles, kindness, and
harmless cheerfulness, he can still think with complacency; and he
hopes that if his little work should fall into the hands of a reader of
that class in whose language it is written, it would not be likely to
damp his love of God, or slacken the tone of his moral sentiment, or
lower the dignity of his self-esteem'.[43] Barnes' whole artistic and

---

[41] Baxter p.252. "It was this love...that gave him so much sympathy with his
people as a priest".

[42] Alan Chedzoy, *Poems Grave and Gay*, Afterword, p.xx

[43] *Poems of Rural Life in the Dorset Dialect*, p.48

aesthetic sense, his sense of 'tastecraft' and 'fairhoodlore' was dictated by his love for what he wrote of. 'A scorn of the subject produces satire, therefore satire, however clever, is no more true Art than a caricature is an artistic painting'. 'He did not study his subjects merely as subjects for his poems... but he entered into their lives and feelings, saw their sorrows as they saw them, laughed in their joys as they laughed, for his heart remained to his old age simple as the heart of a child, though his head was stored with the lore of a sage'.[44] Thus he would generally avoid unpleasant themes, he wanted to show the best in man – what was loveable in him. Some have doubted that what he described was real, it seems too rosy-hued, but Barnes assured that what he described was all real – he simply avoided the unpleasant as unedifying: 'Many persons thought that he had painted our folk in too bright colours, but everything which he had written was true of someone in the classes described in the poems; he was painting, in fact, from life, though the level might be somewhat above the average'.[45] And even when he did mention social problems in his artistic work, his poetry, it was always with compassion. Such is the case of his poems 'The Lovechild', concerning illegitimacy, or 'The Child an the Mowers', concerning the accidental death of a child, one of his own brothers. In other words it was Barnes' goal always to edify the reader, whether in the actual story he was describing, or his choice of rhyme and language. Barnes had great taste and it is of this that he wrote in his most important statement on Art in *Thoughts on Art and Beauty* which we shall now examine.[46]

In this quite lengthy article which we shall quote from in some considerable detail, Barnes puts into words his vision, which is a deeply religious one, of Beauty. He begins by his own definition of Beauty in Nature and Art; 'The beautiful in Nature is the unmarred result of God's first creative or forming will, and that the beautiful in

---

[44] Baxter, p.252
[45] op. cit., p.322
[46] All the following quotations, unless otherwise indicated, are all taken from, 'Thoughts on Beauty and Art', in *Macmillan's Magazine* June 1861, pp.126-137.

Art is the result of an unmistaken working of man in accordance with the beautiful in Nature'. By 'God's first creative or forming will' Barnes explains that he means the Creation as God intended it to be, and not as man has made it through his interference in it, in other words, he means the Creation in a pristine, Edenic form, before the Fall. His vision is one of Paradise. He explains that, even in his own time: 'There is yet so much of the beauty of God's primary work, that our minds can well rise from their marred shapes to the higher ones, or the beau ideal, of which they may be spoilt forms; and that beau ideal is, in our opinion, one of the true objects of high art... We may gather from choice forms of manhood, as well as womanhood, enough of beauty to conceive the good of God's first work'. He goes on to identify the beautiful with the good – we are a long way from the empty aestheticism of the decadent end of the nineteenth century – Barnes aesthetic sense has a moral purpose; beauty is moral beauty. 'In the first chapter of Genesis, we read that God saw everything that he had made, and, behold, it was very good – where the Hebrew word for good, 'tov', means, also, beautiful; as in the Septuagint [Greek] it is given by the word 'kalà', beautiful. The beautiful is also the good by reason of a fitness or harmony which it possesses'. From this point on Barnes defines what he means by fitness or harmony. And here we enter into the world of observation of Nature and Art of a most insightful and thoughtful man.

Thus he links beauty in Creation with usefulness: a man with disproportionate limbs would be neither comely nor fitted to carry out physical work; in Nature each tree has its own form of trunk, adapted to the weight of branches above it. In architecture man must learn to do likewise: 'God's rule of no waste, no want is a pattern for us in our buildings. A heavy building or roof on slender pillars of lead or brick would be unhandsome, even if they should stand by side strokes, and uphold their weight'. In other words in Nature, and therefore by human imitation in Art, the spiritual and the practical, the beautiful and the functional must be joined together. This is very reminiscent of William Morris who believed that the useful and the beautiful should be as one. Barnes saw the same beauty in numerical symmetry; a man with only one limb or eye is not as handsome as one with two. This theme of harmonic proportion he had already developed in a letter published in 1843, 'On Harmonic Proportion in Churches'.[47] Using the three numbers 6, 3 and 2, used in the architecture of Solomon's Temple, he suggested that these numbers, or 'harmonic triad' as he called them, be applied to the relative heights of church tower, nave and chancel. Similarly another harmonic triad would be made by the ground-widths of nave, chancel and tower. These same ideas of harmony and proportion he applied to form and colour in house-building. Thus he felt the need to find harmonic proportion for rectangles which occur in houses and parts of houses – windows, door-frames, room-sides, tables, boxes, books, bookcases and pictures. As a picture restorer and framer himself, Barnes knew from experience what he was talking about and indeed even wrote on the subject of picture-framing.

He also found harmony and beauty in the curves of Nature: 'The circle in the earth's sky-line [horizon], and in the sun and moon, and the daily path-bows [orbits] of the heavenly bodies; in the fungi at our feet, and the blossoms of flowers, and the stems of plants; in a falling drop of rain, and the circle of the out-smitten water on the casting of a stone into a pool, You cannot fill a bag but that it swells into a circle; and the circle glows in the rainbow... You cannot cast a stone, or strike a ball, or send a shot through the air, but that its path shall be a determinate curve of the truest form... Look for pleasure at the line of beauty, and other curves of charming grace in the wind-blown stems of grass, and bowing barley or wheat; in the water-shaken bulrush, in the leaves of plants, and in the petals of flowers; in the outlines of birds, and even their feathers and eggs... the flight-curves of the swallow and lark, the slow swim of the cloud, the giddy whirl of the foam at the pool... the curling of the wreath of smoke, the reeling barley, and the rocking tree, are all cases of curve-motions, and are all beautiful'. A similar harmony and beauty is present, he said, in colour. Nature is full, says Barnes, of juxtapositions of colour, 'in flowers and birds, in trees and butterflies, plants and blossom, in

---

[47] *Gentleman's Magazine* December 1843, p.574

insects and egg-shells, in the sea and the sand. These are not by chance, but evidence of the God's 'first forming will'. He states that these are colours to be imitated by man in decoration. 'Nature is the best School of Art, and of Schools of Art among men those are the best that are Nature's best interpreters'. Here again in this almost sacramental vision of Nature and Art we are surely reminded of William Morris, writing later than Barnes: 'Decoration should remind you of something beyond itself, of something of which it is but a visible symbol'.

The combination of shape, line and colour is found in landscape and Barnes deems most beautiful 'hills and slopes, and winding valleys, with hanging woods, and falling streams'. The green of the earth, and the blue of the sky, of which the world affords us such breadths, are less wearisome and destructive to the sight than would be a world of red or white'. 'In all these beautiful things there is fitness [usefulness] – fitness of water to irrigate growth, and to run for all lips to the sea'. Observantly he points out: 'the lower limbs of our meadow trees are mostly so high from the ground as to afford head-room for cattle or man in need of shade or shelter, are thus in harmony with cattle and man'. He gives other instances of this fundamental intuition of the natural combination of beauty and good, of loveliness and usefulness: 'A winding stream is felt to be more beautiful than a straight ditch', states Barnes, and then goes on to explain that because a stream winds it drains a greater area of ground and more efficiently. This then is Barnes' basic intuition as regards Nature which he goes on to extend it to Art.

'It is the office of high art to seek and show to man the pure forms of God's untarnished earthly good', says Barnes of the role and purpose of Art. He also quoted from his beloved Welsh triads: 'The three main things necessary for a man of artistic genius are an eye to see Nature, a heart to feel Nature, and boldness to follow Nature', and: 'There are three men on whom everyone should look with esteem – one who looks with love on the face of the earth, on works of Art, and on little children'. We can surely apply both of these triads to Barnes himself. It is for these reasons that Barnes denies that photography can ever be part of high Art, which 'always looks from marred to unmarred beauty; while photography must take blemished with primary good'. Barnes sees a moral purpose in Art – its task is to seek out beauty and therefore good. This is why he rejoices in the interest in Art in towns, 'where much of the beautiful in Nature must be far forlorn [lost] by many of working people'. In other words where Nature is obscured, the loss can in some way be made up for by Art. Art must however be faithful to a religious function, not a commercial one; artists must be honest. Today, says Barnes, this is no longer the case: 'The old workmen were faithful and wrought to God, or art, or conscience, rather than to Pluto... Our age is one of falsehood and sham', and he refers to the use of veneer, plaster, paste, cloth, coatings – mere imitations to camouflage the shoddiness of industrial civilisation. 'Nature and true Art, however, are faithful, and he adds: 'There will be no Art where the workman panders to a low taste or deceives men rather than instructs them in the truth; and there is no high aim but the beautiful. Follow Nature: work to her truth'. This latter phrase Barnes repeated often throughout his life and in many ways it sums up his vision of the role and purpose of Art – to follow Nature, for Nature contained the Beauty of God's Creation. Indeed Barnes concludes his article in *Macmillan's Magazine* with the following words which will surely find echoes among many today: 'Let those who follow Art work on in faith, with the high aim of winning, at first, excellence rather than money... where money is the first aim, the higher one may never be reached. The object of high Art is the doing of good to men's minds'.

Barnes' artistic values and ideals were then the result of his rural origins and closeness to Nature. 'He loved Nature and he loved Art, but he hated artificiality in any form whatsoever'.[48] For him all great and true Art followed Nature. This was a religious instinct, for he saw not in Nature some wild and untamed force, but rather the Hand of the Creator. Barnes saw in Nature the Garden of Eden, Nature as God intended it to be before the Fall. Barnes' vision was paradisiac. This explains why he was opposed to any sort of artifice, why Art itself had to 'follow Nature', because, since it was the work of God, it was

---

[48] Dugdale, p.190

beautiful and good. Its beauty was in form and colour, its goodness in its practical usefulness. Nature then, being the shadow of God's beauty, was the work of love and this was why true Art, according to Barnes, was also the work of love: 'There is no Art without love'. As one of his admirers, E. M. Forster, wrote: 'He gathered up all the happiness and beauty around him'.[49] The purpose of Nature and Art (and Science too[50]) was to lead man to the discovery (or rather recovery) of the presence of God around him, to Faith. Through the observation and contemplation of Nature, which he so much practised himself,[51] man, said Barnes, could discover the imprint of the Creator and the presence of the Divine would be revealed, thus humbling man's mind, and not, in Darwinian fashion, puffing it up with the pride of illusory, false knowledge gained in the absence of Faith. From the examination of Creation, or the imitation of it through Art, man's mind would be raised up to contemplate the Wisdom of the Creator, the harmony and beauty of the Divine Wisdom. And Barnes' own mind, from childhood on and throughout his life, rose to contemplate that very Wisdom and Beauty.

---

[49] E. M. Forster: Homage to William Barnes, *New Statesman and Nation*, 9/12/1939, pp.819-20.

[50] "The task of the scientist, considered Barnes, was to reveal God's laws in the material world, as he himself had sought such laws in Science, Art, Language, Social Economics and Education". (See Hearl, p.299)

[51] As a teacher and excellent pedagogue Barnes was very keen on what we would now call 'field trips'. He also thought sport necessary and was especially keen on cricket (See Hearl, p.185). At home he would spend hours in his garden lost in the contemplation of Nature.

Chapter 4

Marriage

O woman, heart-enthralling queen
Of fairest beings eyes have ever seen,
In thee a loving God bestows
The best of blessings man e'er knows;

William Barnes, Athelhamton House

One thing that William Barnes could never be accused of is misogyny. Aged eighteen, he fell in love with his future 'loveworthy and ever-beloved wife' at first sight and adored her the rest of his life, and as we can imagine, into eternity. Indeed, after her death, he closed each day's entry in his diary with her name. Of his Julia he wrote, 'Her every place was joy'. As he wrote in his poem, 'A Wife A-Prais'd': 'Your smilen feäce ha' been my jaÿ; Your soul o' greäce ha' been my jaÿ'. His marriage was infinitely happy, this part of his life was domestic bliss. In his poem 'Fatherhood', he wrote: 'the hands ov a wife an' a child Be the blessens ov low or ov high'. He was a natural husband and father, a family man in every possible sense. In one poem 'The Bean Vield', he gives the impression that a man in love is one who can forget all the troubles of the world:

Since there do come drough yonder hatch,
An' bloom below the house's thatch,
The best o'maidens, an' do own
That she is mine, an' mine alwone:
Zoo I can zee that love do gi'e
The best ov all good gifts to me.

A phrenological sketch of his character made some twelve years after her death describes Barnes as, 'of rather warm and amative feelings and a thoroughly family and domestic man – strong in paternal love and in all domestic attachment. He is fond of home and country and all his warmest affections concentrate around the domestic hearth.

The dearest spot to him is the Englishman's fireside, to him there is in reality, 'No place like Home'.[52] And he himself wrote: 'The home, when he is himself a father, is the nest in which he feels happy to shield his own beloved offspring from the threatening harms of the welkin and the wild... and the 'hearth' of the English home, where the Christian Englishman, blest with his daily bread, hallows his house to God by daily thanksgiving, that he has everything that is truly needful in his earthly life; and while he therefore loves his home, he still bears in mind that it is not his home for ever... and labours to win the house not made by hands'.[53] The word 'hwome' is indeed very common in his poems, an example is his poem, 'Home's a Nest': '...Home's a Nest, Where our children are bred to fulfil Not our own, but our Father's good will'. Barnes' idyll, combining the country and the countrywoman, was that of the 'Woakland Dell', where:

> Noo coaches' wheels, wi' glitt'ren spwokes,
> Do roll on there wi' high-born vo'ks,..
> Zoo happy I, if you mid dwell,
> Wi' me down where the clote [water-lily] do blow
> Upon the stream a-winden slow,
> Among the woaks in woak-tree dell.

Barnes would definitely have called his wife his better half; many of his poems praise women, for example 'The Maid That I Have Won' or 'True Love'. The failure of his school in Dorchester can ultimately be attributed to the death of Julia ten years before. Poems such as 'Plorata Veris Lachrymis', 'The Wife A-Lost', 'My Dearest Julia', 'My Dearest Wife', 'The Wold Wall', 'The Leady's Tower', 'The Trial Past' and 'Woak Hill' are eloquent witness to his devastation on Julia's death. But perhaps the most remarkable thing, so far overlooked by all commentators, is that in his youth William Barnes had foreseen just this possibility in his poem 'A Giulia':

---

[52] Quoted in Chedzoy, *William Barnes*, p.156
[53] *Views of Labour and Gold* p.179

And shall I first from mortal life depart,
And leave my dearest Giulia here behind?
Or wilt thou fly from me? Ah! who can tell.
But thou art now so dear to my heart,
That wert thou gone from me, I could not find
A joy without thee: this I know full well.

For him man was only half of humankind – woman the other half,
just as important, but in a different way. Thus in a religious poem,
almost a hymn, 'For a Marriage', he wrote:

For so the minds of man, and bride,
So meetly match'd by God's own plan,
Would seem far less two sundry minds,
Than sides of one full mind of man.
For one is fine, where one is coarse;
If one is hard, there one is meek;
For one too shrinking, one is bold;
And one is strong, where one is weak.

His beliefs as regards family life and men and women would today be
called traditional, even perhaps reactionary, but we would suggest
that they are far subtler and deeper than a superficial glance might
suggest.

In his *Views of Labour and Gold* (henceforth referred to as VLG), he
says: 'The Allwise Himself has willed some division of skill by the
sexes, though our division of it has now in some cases, thwarted what
has been deemed to be the Divine plan. It seems as if man had in his
hands the defence of his life and rights, and the winning of food, as
by hunting, farming, and handicrafts and commerce; and that woman
was to hold the lighter indoor works of a fine hand guided by fancy,
the making of apparel, and the adorning of the abode; and so our
Saxon speech seems to have been quite right, when, on the pen of
King Alfred, it called the male sex the spear sex, and women the
spindle sex; and when it called a wife 'seo wif', the weaver, or 'seo
wifman', the weaving man, and a girl 'a spinster', as in those times
women were the makers of the outer adornings of the body, while

men were handlers of the spear'.[54] 'The mother of Alfred, like other ladies of old, is said to have been skilful in spinning, and to have trained her daughters to the same work; and Edward the Elder, set his sons to school, and his daughters to wool-work'.[55] Such views would seem perfectly normal in a pre-industrial society, to us they may raise eyebrows and the old stereotypes of the tyrannical man with his oppressed wife locked away in the house may come to mind. But that is not what Barnes is saying, that would be to put modern stereotypes into Barnes' mind. What did he really mean?

Firstly Barnes sees women as complementary to men: 'Do not begin with the thought that the minds of the man and woman are of the same cast, or that one is higher than the other, neither is the higher, but they differ that each may be the best for its mission, and each has that which the other lacks, and both make together the one full mind of mankind'.[56] Although he did not believe that one sex was 'higher' than another, equality between the sexes would not have been his first thought. Nevertheless he does mention the question of equality and treats it sympathetically but without actually committing himself on the subject: 'From time to time we meet with opinions on the rights of women – such as that they have fewer than those of men, and that they ought to have more than the law has allowed them, and as many as those of men, since they are, in truth, and should be holden [held] by the law, every way equal to man'.[57] In spite of this clear sympathy as regards the question of equality, Barnes' first thought would seem rather to have been the differences between the sexes; otherwise how could there be any complementarity between them, or for that matter, any attraction? He spoke of 'the true work, mindly as well as bodily, of woman's calling; and her fittedness for it in her very unlikeness to man... each fulfils the work of help meet for the other'. 'In wedlock there

---

[54] op. cit. p.80
[55] 'Christian Marriage' in *The Ladies' Treasury (LT)* April 1866, p.197
[56] Baxter, p.282
[57] *LT* March 1866, p.138

is in the union of the man and woman, a full mind-life'.[58] He saw man's role in tilth [agriculture], defence, hand [manual] work and trade. Woman's calling is in the home; he expressed this in a charming poem, 'The Sky A-Clearen', where he speaks of 'maïdens' who:

> But have noo call to spweil [spoil] their looks
> By work, that God could never meäke
> Their weaker han's to underteäke,
> Though skies mid be a-cleären.
> Tis wrong vor women's han's to clips [clasp]

> The zull [plough] an' reap-hook, speades an' whips;
> An' men abroad [outside], should leave, by right,
> Woone [One] faithful heart at hwome to light
> Their bit o'vier [fire] up at night...

And in another poem, 'Don't Ceare', he wrote: 'Though the storm do beat down on my poll [head], Ther's a wife-brighten'd vier [fire] at the end o' my road, An' her love vor the jay [joy] o' my soul'. Barnes wrote: 'Woman is to be the queen of man's home... or light of the house... In Tonga the men say it is not feminine, or fit for women, to do hard work, and they do not like a masculine woman... men take on themselves those heavy and rough tasks which are unfit for the softer sex... The setting of women on [heavy, physical] work... threatens evil to her bodily and social state, since it blunts her refinement'.[59]

Having then explained why he is opposed to woman's doing of rough, physical work – because it blunts her refinement – he goes on to explain this concept. Woman, he writes in a poem, must lead man 'to rise above Unworthy deeds to win her love'.[60] Woman is, 'to refine man and the world... if woman is to be the refiner of man, and if there cannot be high refinement without aesthetics or things that belong to fine feelings in the world of loveworthy things, so she

---

[58] *LT* February 1866, p.82
[59] *LT* April 1866, p.197
[60] 'Athelhamton House' (poem)

herself must have a love of those things for which she is to work, 'ta kala', things of beauty... Few men have woman's lovesomeness [affection].[61] Part of this refining, according to Barnes, should be in woman's dress, and he pleaded that girls should not cut their hair short and should dress becomingly: 'Man has to do the rough work of life and it tends to make him coarse, harsh, animal, Godless... but woman is the refiner of his rudeness, the purifier of his affection and his abode. Therefore let girls' minds be trained to choose becoming attire'.[62] This refinement of woman, her greater ability to love and ennoble is linked with the fact that God 'made woman what a true woman is, that she too often believes with the heart rather than the head'.[63] This he connects with another, and now very topical issue: "On withholding women from the ministry, the Apostolic Constitutions say, 'Our Lord who sent us out to teach the people and the heathen never sent forth women to preach, although he could have found them... If therefore, it were needful that women should preach, He himself would have bidden these women with us to instruct the people'."[64] He saw woman's role elsewhere: 'The finer make of woman, and her keener feelings, mark her for offices finer than the true ones of the more hardy man... Another office of woman, as such, is the refinement of the world, or of man. The farther-cast thoughts and the wider-planned works of man, his stern toils in war, his heavier work, his coarser businesses, and his needful off-calledness from hallowed or refined forms of life, tend to lower the tone of his mind towards brutishness'.[65] 'Upon women hang the moral life and political strength of the nation... The good mother gives her child, under God, more than his physical frame, for she moulds his soul also. From a generation of bad mothers no nation can ever hope for a generation of good men. While our girls are being unwomaned... morally spoilt in the factory and the field... the statesman wonders why their children are so degenerate and

---

[61] *LT* p.83
[62] Quoted Hearl, pp.240-1
[63] *LT* p.196
[64] op. cit.
[65] *LT* p.82

demoralised!'.[66] 'If we cannot save our women we are all lost'.[67] Referring to the Holy Virgin Mary, the Mother of God, he wrote: 'Woman is God's own teacher'.[68] Barnes goes on then to speak of the mutual duties of spouses and the duties of men, of whom he is also exacting.

First of all he sees for men and women only one natural destiny – marriage. In one poem, 'Thatchen o' the Rick', he wrote: 'An noo good man in ouer land Think lightly o' the wedden band [bond]'. His poetry refers many times to the importance and happiness of marriage, for example in 'The Bachelor' ('Dine alwone! Pine alwone! Whine alwone! Oh! what a life!' I'll have a friend in a wife'), 'In the Spring', 'Fatherhood' , 'A Good Father', 'Childern's Childern'. In one poem, however, 'The Love Child', Barnes movingly expresses his compassion for the fate of a child born out of wedlock – 'Oh! a God-gift a-treated wi' scorn' – he was no hard-hearted, hypocritical prig. In another poem, 'Week's End in Zummer in the Wold Vo'k's Time', he spoke of another maiden undone who had drowned herself from shame. His sympathies were obviously with her and not the man. Indeed, at a time when such issues were hardly mentioned, Barnes even wrote to the Press urging aid for desperate unmarried and deserted mothers, demanding that fathers be forced to pay maintenance. Another common theme in his poems was the jilted maiden, for instance in 'Jane of Buckley-Hill', 'Rose of Farrancoombe', 'Hope A-Left Behind'. Referring to marriages of reason, made for money, where, as was common among the wealthy of the nineteenth century, women would be kept in 'costly idleness' and men would only marry for a generous dowry, he wrote: 'God's true wedlock, grounded on the love of excellence and loveworthiness, is often lost, and in its stead we have a train of evils, physical and moral, which are increasing at a frightful rate'.[69] Elsewhere he warns that: 'St. Paul himself (1 Tim. 4,3) says that one of the misteachings

---

[66] *Gentlemen's Magazine* October 1848, pp.401-2
[67] Quoted Hearl, pp.240-1
[68] op. cit.
[69] *VLG* p.97

of times when men should fall off from the faith, giving heed to seducing spirits and doctrines of devils, should be that of forbidding to marry'.[70] Clearly Barnes' attitude to divorce is conservative, seeing in it the potentially disastrous consequences of the vicious circle: 'The more readily the law affords divorce the more recklessly may men form unhappy marriages for lust or money; and it may be that much of the unhappiness in which some may find the foregoing need of divorce may be the consequence of it'.[71] Having spoken then of woman's role and marriage in general what does Barnes have to say of man's role in marriage?

Barnes sees man's role as noble and self-sacrificing and is strongly opposed to any tyranny on the part of a husband: 'The tyrannical wielding of man's strength over women's yieldingness has been always deemed a shame to manhood... The honouring and shielding of women was, and will always be, the glory of... noble minds... the great rule was never to hurt, in deed or word, a woman, nor a man in woman's company'.[72] That man should be the head of a family 'is not a slavish subjection is clear, as the husband vows to honour, as well as to love, comfort, and keep the wife'.[73] And he says as much in a number of poems, 'Treat Well Your Wife' or 'The Broken Heart', where he calls men to look after their wives. We are far here from the feminist stereotype of the oppressive male, but close to the concept of the supportive husband and father.

In truth, what Barnes offers is not a patriarchal society, but rather a patriarchal *and* matriarchal society. What he wanted was a return to the state of men and women, and therefore family life, found in Saxon society, that life found in pre-Conquest England. This has been studied in considerable detail over the years, one of the finest works on the subject being Doris Stenton's groundbreaking study 'The English Woman in History', where she concluded: 'The evidence that survives from Anglo-Saxon England indicates that women were then

---

[70] *LT* p.83
[71] *LT* p.260
[72] *LT* March 1866, p.138
[73] *LT* p.196

more nearly the equal companions of their husbands and brothers than at any other period before the modern age. In the higher ranges of society this rough and ready partnership was ended by the Norman Conquest, which introduced into England a military society... it must be confessed that the teaching of the medieval (i.e. post-Conquest) Church reinforced the subjection which feudal law imposed on all wives'.[74] And a more recent study, 'Women in Anglo-Saxon England and the Impact of 1066', points out that:'... the impact of the Norman Conquest... is almost instantly followed by the impact of the Gregorian reform, when theological concept hardens into canon law, and canon law acquires control of much legislation concerning women. The combination of the new military-based civil law and the increasing effectiveness of anti-female canon law was very sharply differentiated from that in the pre-1066 era... the study of women in Anglo-Saxon England is not complete without demonstrating the complete shift of pattern, the turn of the tide, within a single century after 1066'.[75] Thus Old English women held property, could be independent of men. Some Old English Abbesses were in charge of double monasteries, ruling over nuns and monks. The situation changed dramatically and barbarously after the Conquest – at least among the aristocracy ('the higher ranges of society') – since they were Normans in origin, when women were more or less deprived of rights and kept to be used by men. However for the English peasantry nothing at all changed, and this is exactly what the pre-industrial values of Barnes were linked with – pre-Conquest values. They had lasted, at least in the Dorset countryside, until the nineteenth century and the coming of urbanisation with the Industrial Revolution. And Barnes was more of an eighteenth century man, for he had known the time before the Enclosures, before Industry and the railways, before the agglomeration of farms into large units, before the first industrialisation of Agriculture. He had known the time of the smallholder and yeoman-farmer, the heirs of the folk-life of the

---

[74] D. Stenton, *The English Woman in History*, Epilogue, London 1957
[75] Christine Fell, *Women in Anglo-Saxon England and the Impact of 1066*, p.14, London 1984

Saxon English. William Barnes was not talking from books, he had actually lived in that patriarchal/matriarchal society – and found it a successful one. Small wonder that Lady Stenton began her book with a chapter on 'Anglo-Saxon Woman' and ended it with 'Reaction and the Rise of Modern Feminism'.

Since folklore and folk-life was one of Barnes' interests, we could do no better than add to this survey of his views on men and women, marriage and family life, by quoting some of the many 'ring-posies' that he collected and published in 'The Ladies' Treasury'.[76] Now a ring posy is a short verse traditionally engraved on a wedding-ring and Barnes collected over 150 of them, most of which went back to the seventeenth century and before. We shall quote here a selection of them:

'Godly love will not remove'.
'United hearts death only partes'.
'My promise past shall ever last'.
'Virtue passeth riches'.
'Live in love, and fear the Lord'.
'We join our love in Christ above'.
'God gives increase to love and peace'.
'God's blessing be on thee and me'.
'God and thee my comfort be'.
'God for me appointed thee'.
'I have obtained what God ordained'.
'God thought fit this knot to knitt'.
'As Christ decreed so we agreed'.
'Where hearts agree, there God will be'.
'In thee my choice, I do rejoice'.
'Let me in thee most happy be'.
'Heart content cannot repent'.
'Live, love and be happy'.
'Thy consent is my content'.

---

[76] *LT* pp.259-62 and 328-9 (May and June 1866)

'Love entire is my desire'.
'God unite our hearts aright'.
'A loving wife, a happy life'.
'God above, keep us in love'.
'In thy sight is my delight'.
'God's Providence is our inheritance'.
'Lord, all our days, direct our ways'.
'If faith ceaseth, love must perish'.
'The Lord us bless with good success'.

That William Barnes collected these posies indicates perhaps more clearly than anything else how exactly he saw marriage. Firstly, marriage had to be not for money but for love – as was his own. Secondly, marriage was nourished by religious faith – as was his own. Thirdly, husband and wife, since they had chosen freely, had to be content with their lots – as he and his wife were. Love, faith and contentment; these are the three words that for Barnes brought domestic bliss.

Perhaps many find Barnes' views very out-of-date. We must remember that he wrote some six generations ago – the Dorset priest-poet wrote for a society that had only just entered the Industrial Revolution. Certainly today, when few work on the land, when men and women receive the same education and social conditioning, in an age of equal opportunities, when working couples are the norm, we may think Barnes old-fashioned. But perhaps his views of domesticity, each partner assuming differing responsibilities in complementarity, is not so old-fashioned. In today's post-industrial society, in the age of the tele-home, the tele-worker and the tele-commuter, where the home has assumed a new importance, perhaps we can learn something from Barnes pre-industrial vision. Certainly Barnes' own marriage was blissfully happy and blessed with six adult and successful children. In comparison, our society, where virtually one marriage in two ends in divorce, one child in five does not live with its father and many lone parents struggle to bring up children on Social Security, many might well conclude that certainly something somewhere is seriously wrong. Surely Barnes' patriarchal and matriarchal vision, the mother assuming her responsibilities, the father nobly sacrificing himself for his wife and family, surely his vision and way of life, provide us with food for thought – and, who knows, perhaps even some answers.

Chapter 5

Society

Ill fares the land, to hastening ills a prey,
Where wealth accumulates, and men decay.

Oliver Goldsmith, *The Deserted Village*

The enclosing of the commons robbed the country folk in England of leisure and independence, the coming of the factories took them from the fields and the old communities, and flung them into the new ones, which were allowed to grow up anyhow, without art, without thought, without faith or hope or charity, till the face of the land was blackened, and the soul of the land under a cloud.

John Masefield, *St. George and the Dragon*

As we have already seen from the two previous chapters, Barnes' values were to a great extent shaped by his upbringing in the Blackmore Vale. True of his artistic values, his attitude to Nature and to Art, true of his attitudes to Marriage, this is also true of all his social values. His fathers and forefathers had all been rooted in the land, the pre-Enclosure, pre-industrial rural way of life. Indeed, despite moving to Dorchester, Barnes later bought (thanks to his wife's frugality, as he acknowledges) a small piece of land in the Vale, as recorded in his poem, 'I Got Two Vields', thus somehow joining his forebears in their way of life. His forefathers were yeomen, self-reliant, self-sufficient, self-improved and self-educated smallholders – like Barnes himself. Barnes, as Hardy said, was a great example of self-help, a genius who had risen from nowhere. He was in favour of self-help not, however, for the sake of money or greed but for the sake of self-respect.

Barnes expressed his social views in several works and poems quite outspokenly. Notably he opposed the Enclosures in several Eclogues such as, 'The Common A-Took-in', 'The Times', 'The 'Lotments',

'Two Farms in Woone', 'Father Come Hwome' or 'The New Poor Laws' and in a poem 'The Leane'. Despite being disguised in dialect and in imitation of Virgil's Eclogues, these poems were in fact quite radical political statements – they were written after rioting among farmworkers, especially in Dorset, and at the time of the injustices inflicted on the Dorset Tolpuddle Martyrs in 1834. As regards emigration for example, even in the form of transportation, Barnes considered it unfair that criminals could emigrate, whereas honest farmworkers, living in conditions of starvation, could not. Of this he wrote in one Eclogue, 'Rusticus Emigrans', where a desperate labourer says, 'If 'twerden var [it weren't for] my children and my wife, I wou'dent gi' zixpence var my life'.

His Eclogues especially have led several commentators to compare Barnes with Cobbett.[77] But Barnes, though often *radical* was not at all a *Radical*, if anything his views could be compared to those of Ruskin and Morris, with the important difference that Barnes preceded them – he was a forerunner. In fact Barnes would have agreed with Cowper: 'God made the country, man made the town'. The mere thought of what men had done in towns saddened him: 'Many a plain wall rises between the workman and the glory of the passing sun, and has shut out his window-framed piece of blue sky, and the cheering whiteness of the flying cloud. Many a day of smoke has blackened the clearness of the sweet spring-tide; many a bright-leaved tree has heretofore given way to crowded shades of narrowed rooms. Many a rood of flowery sward has become rattling streets, where for songs of birds, they have the din of hammers. Many a cheek has been paled, and lovely piece of childhood marred, by longsome hours of over-work'.[78] He found it unnatural that man should work by night and sleep by day; in the country, 'we don't grow up pe,le an' weak But we do work wi' health an' strength' ('Sleep Did Come Wi' The Dew'). And in 'Open Vields' he wrote:

---

[77] For Comparisons with Cobbett, see especially Ruffell, pp.227-30 and Wrigley, 'William Barnes and the Social Problem', *Dorset Natural History and Archaeological Society, Proceedings for 1977*, pp.19-27.

[78] Thoughts on Beauty and Art, *Macmillan's Magazine* June 1861, p.134.

Well, you mid keep the town an' street,
Wi' grassless stwones to beät your veet,
An' zunless windows where your brows
Be never cool'd by swaÿen boughs;
An' let me end, as I begun,
My days in open aïr an' zun.

Barnes was a traditionalist, yearning for the pre-industrial past which he had known in his childhood.[79] And here he professed a certain regional patriotism, for Dorset after all had for long been bypassed by the Industrial Revolution, remaining uncontaminated by grasping industrialism. There was no doubt in Barnes' mind that the country was superior to the town, and he expressed it in poems like 'Praise O' Do'set', 'Farmer's Sons' or 'The Farmer's Woldest Da'ter' [Oldest Daughter], 'Blackmwore Maidens', 'John Bloom in Lon'on' or 'My Orcha'd in Linden Lea'. But in reality it is implicit in his whole work, both poetry and prose. In general he could not understand why the vital activity of agriculture was not more highly valued. If then we are to look at Barnes' social values, we are to look first at his critique of the new nineteenth century society, the urbanised society of the Industrial Revolution.

Perhaps the first tangible results of the changes that came to Dorset were the Enclosures and the merging of farms. The enclosures effectively pauperised the rural classes, for farms were brought up by a few large owners and as a result, 'now they don't imploy so many men Upon the land as work'd upon it then', as Barnes wrote in his Eclogue, 'Two Farms in Woone'. This merging of farms meant the capitalisation and industrialisation of farming. Barnes defined such merging as: 'The kindness which is done by capital when it affords employment to people from whom, by a monopoly, it has taken over their little business is such as one might do to a cock by adorning his head with a plume of feathers pulled out of his own tail'.[80] The aim of the merging of farms was not to continue the traditional,

---

[79] Colloms, p.129 and Forsyth, especially pp.147-50.
[80] *VLG* p.69

contented, self-supporting, village community, but to maximise output and profits at its expense. It also took away any opportunity and motivation for the thrifty labourer to save enough to one day work his own farm, a theme that was close to Barnes' heart and as early as 1829 he had written to the Dorset County Chronicle speaking of this. Poverty and distress grew and Barnes talked of it quite openly. Thus in 'The Hwomestead a-Vell [Fallen] Into Hand', where out of eight farms only three were left, he wrote:

> An' all the happy souls they ved
> Be scattered vur [far] an' wide.
> An' zome o'm [some of them] be a-wanten bread,
> Zome, better off, ha' died,

This can be compared with the former state of the smallholder, for example in his poem, 'The Hwomestead':

> An' I be happy wi' my spot
> O' freehold ground an' mossy cot,
> An' shoulden get a better lot
> If I had all my will.
> I'm landlord o' my little farm,
> I'm king 'ithin my little pleäce;
> I don't break laws, an' don't do harm,
> An' ben't [aren't] afeärd o' noo man's feäce.

[At this point it might be worthwhile making a small digression: if Barnes thought this of the result of the merging of smallholdings in the nineteenth century, what would he have thought of the unemployment caused by the emergence of multinational corporations since the Second World War, the takeover and merger fever since the 1960's, the advent of the Superstore, or for that matter the development of customs unions, fashionably called 'trading blocs', with their 'single markets'?].

Barnes saw the baneful effects of the Enclosures and industrialisation in the rise in crime-rates in his own day, as we have seen in the above-quoted 'The Hwomestead'. In his 'Views of Labour and Gold' he demonstrated statistically that crime actually rose in proportion as farms grew in size. Of the impossibility for the labourer to better himself by saving and starting his own 'farmling', he said: 'The result is that the possession of property, whether to a large or small amount, retains a man from breaking the laws of his country'.[81] He went on to demonstrate that crime rose even more with urbanisation, quoting statistics for Liverpool and Manchester, where the amount of crime was 'ten times that which prevails in the yeomanry counties'.[82] Since Barnes considered that much crime was a result of poor social conditions, it was to some extent a social responsibility. But, having said this, we should not think of Barnes as some kind of 'softee'. Barnes was never negligent and considered leniency to criminals a great mistake. Wrongdoers had to be punished, the innocent had to be protected. There was no reason to be kind to rogues, all had to see that honesty paid, and he thought it unmerciful to the victim to leave the wrong done to him unrighted. However, with his usual balance Barnes was not only against punishment out of cruel vengefulness, but also against the do-gooder who pays more attention to attempting to reform the criminal than to helping the victim. Although Barnes understood the responsibility of society, he also understood the importance of personal responsibility for one's acts.[83] Indeed this same notion of personal responsibility and self-discipline or moral training was the very foundation of his pacific teaching methods.

Some of Barnes' social thought is contained in articles he wrote for the local *Poole and Dorset Herald* in 1849, under the collective title, 'Humilis Domus', subtitled, 'Some thoughts on the Abodes, Life and Social Condition of the Poor, especially in Dorsetshire'. (Some of these thoughts were reprinted later in his *Views of Labour and Gold*). Here he raised a critique against the social changes in English society at the time. Objecting to the National Debt, he considered that its existence causes every worker to have to work longer hours in order to pay it off. Although Barnes was hardly opposed to work as such, he did object to overwork, 'workaholism' as we might now call it.

---

[81] op. cit. pp.71-2
[82] op. cit. pp.72-3
[83] *Notes on Ancient Britain*, pp.73-8

The overworked had no time for his family and children, '...no time to solace himself with the gifts of God... no time to enlighten and purify his soul by a peaceful reading of the word of life... While moderate labour is wholesome to the body and good to the mind, excessive daily toil is fraught with evil to the body and soul... The holy affection of kindred for kindred grows out of the happier hours of freedom and rest in house life'.[84] He considered that long working hours were baneful for family life: 'These graces [a happy house-life], therefore, grow out of incidents and services for which some time, with freedom from toil, is needful. Good fathers and mothers (and there are good ones among the poor, and would be more with a happier house-life) are the best teachers of children, and a good home is the best school for the formation of the mind'.[85] Regarding a not unconnected field, slavery, Barnes was of the opinion: 'Slavery is as destructive to its masters as to its slaves'.[86]

On the other hand Barnes was equally against enforced idleness, and would certainly have wanted to replace 'welfare' with 'workfare': 'It is better for paupers themselves that they should do something rather than nothing for their money towards the amelioration of the life of men'.[87] However, he is equally stern with the idle rich, living off unearned income, whom he sees as little more than parasites: 'The consumption of a gay and insolvent spendthrift is most awfully large: his horse and carriage, and wine and grogs, and meats and cigars, and clothing, and firing, and travelling, are all most costly... The consumption of a portion of the nation's wealth by unproductive spendthrifts, and reckless insolvents... is as much a loss to the community as would be the destruction of it by fire, or locusts, or any other unproductive consumer'.[88] 'The Christian law is that if any man

---

[84] *Poole and Dorset Herald* (PDH), 26/4/1849
[85] *VLG* p.171
[86] Professor Charlotte Lindgren in *Proceedings of the William Barnes Society* 1983-92, Vol I, p.43.
[87] PDH 3/5/1849
[88] op. cit. 24/5/1849

will not work, neither should he eat'.[89] Moreover, the existence of the idle rich, said Barnes with prophetical (but much disregarded) common sense, could be politically dangerous: '…in a community of many rich idlers, care should be taken of the honest working classes, or else they will become degraded and dangerous'.[90] Elsewhere[91] he adds: 'Disdain of labour and pride of wealth are breeding among us great evils of social life'. (Some might wonder if these words were really written in 1859 and not perhaps in the 1990s).

Moreover modern industrialism may have produced quantity, but it did not produce quality; modern goods were decadent and shoddy. 'Primitive' peoples in the Sandwich Islands were able, says Barnes, to make clothing of a skill and grace that no machinery could make. And Indians made rush baskets so water-tight that they were waterproof, and Hindu cooks with hardly any tools will cook a better meal that 'will allow little glory to our load of cooking gear'.[92] In poems like 'The Stwonen [Stone] Porch' or 'The Girt Wold [Great Old] House O'Mossy Stwone' he criticised modern buildings, which are too small, do not let sunshine in, have thin deal doors, are made of brick not stone, 'wi' yards a-sprinkled wi' a mop, Too little vor a vrog to hop'. Barnes cries: 'But let me live an' die where I Can zee the ground, an' trees, an' sky'. On the same theme Barnes was greatly alarmed at the plight of the poor who were badly housed and considered it only natural that every family have its own house and that the children of each sex have its own room.[93] Worse still was the fate of those who went to the workhouse, where orphans lived in misery and where wives were separated from husbands contrary to Christian marriage: 'They mid [might] as well, I think, each wi' his bride Goo back to Church an' have their knot untied', he wrote in 'The New Poor Laws' Barnes' general feeling was that social life was suffering from 'Progress' (a feeling widespread at the end of the

---

[89] *VLG* p.96
[90] op. cit. p.163
[91] op. cit. p.97
[92] op. cit. p.111
[93] op. cit. pp.181-2

twentieth century too): 'I believe that most of our so-called improvements either displace a good, or bring in their train some evil, and that our true progress in well-being is only the difference of good of the so-called improvement and the good displaced by it or the evil which follows it'.[94] He expressed this most effectively and pithily in a poem, 'The Cost of Improvement', written in 'National' English:

> For aught that's nice
> You pay a price...
> The higher has become your speed
> The stronger are your calls for haste;
> Wealth's quicker streams in more ways waste,
> The more you have the more you need.
> Your fathers trode on English dust,
> And while you, o'er the world, will roam,
> The more you roam, the more you must,
> From irksomeness of any home.
> Whatever changes you may choose,
> And something gain, you something lose...
> Fell woods, your shield from wind and heat,
> And you must meet the weather's strokes;
> Or turn the oak-grove to a street,
> And smoking tuns will cost the oaks.
> Give night with day to toil for wealth,
> And then your gain will cost your health.
> To buy new gold
> Give up some old.

We have come across little in the 1990's more pertinent or topical to today's situation than this, written nearly six generations ago.

William Barnes then was very critical of the social results of the processes of industrialisation and urbanisation proceeding in Victorian England. Moreover, he put forward ideas as to where solutions might be found. Firstly, he was resolutely opposed to largeness and agglomerations which he saw as socially and spiritually

---

[94] op. cit. p.155

unhealthy: 'Another evil of congregated labour is... an outfalling from the ordinances of grace... being collected from sundry places, they sink into a godless and dark-minded form of life'.[95] Barnes' ideal, when not in the smallholder or yeoman-farmer, was certainly in cottage industry, the cottage economy: 'The cutting of the Bohemian glass is, I believe, carried on by men who work each in the quiet of his own house, which may be in the pretty nook of a village dell; and the carding and spinning of wool, and buttoning, were formerly home-work in this country'.[96] But who would govern this mass of cottage-workers and peasant-farmers?

In his largely linguistic and historical work of 1869, *Early England and the Saxon-English*, Barnes, speaking of instances of nineteenth century hooliganism, wrote: 'The mindstrength and body worksomeness [mental and physical strength] of the Saxon, which are of great might for good when well spent, need a training in wisdom to keep them from mischief. The Saxon's mind, and above all in the young, is destructive, and his sprackness [energy] wants the guidance of refined thought'.[97] Barnes preached this idea of refining the 'Saxon' mind as part of his lecturing for educational and mutual improvement associations. For example, according to a newspaper report on a lecture given in Corfe (and no doubt repeated elsewhere): 'He reminded those present, as Anglo-Saxons, that (to use a homely expression) they had the 'stuff' in them to make great men, and exhorting them so to study God's Word, and to train their minds they might really become good men, and above all, good Christians'.[98]

In other words Barnes deemed that English folk needed to be governed by some hierarchy. Given that in any society, a hierarchy is inevitable, he came to the logical conclusion that this hierarchy must be enlightened, to justify its privileges, it also had to carry out burdensome but needful duties. His solution was this: 'There should be some classes free of hand-toil [manual work], that they might

---

[95] op. cit. pp.114-5
[96] op. cit. p.115
[97] *Early England and the Saxon English*, pp.63-4.
[98] Scrapbook II, p.32, in the Dorset County Museum

purify and adorn the nobler element of man, their mind, with the graces and excellence of a free and intellectual life, and let their life of intelligence shine for the good of the darker-minded sons of toil. Every community needs men who... might be the better qualified to effect man's well-being either as clergy, legislators, magistrates, lawyers or otherwise... The squire and his lady are a great social good when they live among the poor, and keep before their eyes the graceful pattern of a Christian life, and raise their tone of feeling by kindness and sober bearing'.[99] Barnes hope was then in an enlightened squirearchy. This was not imagination, this was his childhood from which he recalled the toast of the Harvest Home:[100]

> Here's a health unto our meäster,
> The founder of the feäst;
> And I hope to God, wi' all my heart,
> His soul in heaven mid rest.
> That everything mid prosper
> That ever he teäke in hand.
> Vor we be all his sarvants,
> And all at his command.

Indeed he actually portrayed this class in his poetry, for instance in 'Culver Dell and the Squire' (from which, significantly, was taken the verse in praise of Barnes himself on his statue in Dorchester) the squire is one who knows the poor, sympathises with them and above all helps them:

> An' all the vo'k did love so well
> The good wold [old] squire o' Culver dell...
> Vor he did know the poor so well
> 'S [As] the richest vo'k in Culver Dell.

In 'the Leane', written against the Enclosures, the same much respected and loved squire appears again, letting trespassers off with a smile and 'mild words' which 'cut 'em like swords': his authority alone is enough

---

99 *VLG* pp.172-3
100 Baxter, p.7

to shame the lawbreaker. In one of his Eclogues 'The 'Lotments', he again praised the squire: 'Why 'twer the squire, good now! a worthy man, That vu'st [first] brought into ouer pleäce the plan; He zaid he'd let a vew odd eäcres O' land to us poor leäb'ren men'. And in another poem, 'Herrenston', he describes a Christmas party given to villagers by the local Herrenston squire and his good lady:

> Zoo then the leady an' the squier,
> At Chris'mas, gather'd girt [big] an' small,
> Vor me'th [mirth] avore their roaren vier [fire],
> An' roun' their bwoard, 'ithin [within] the hall;...
> Zoo peace betide the girt vo'k's [rich folk's] land,
> When they can stoop, wi' kindly smile,
> An' teake a poor man by the hand,
> An' cheer en [him] in his daily tweil [toil].
> An' oh! mid [might] He that's vur [far] above
> The highest here, reward their love,
> An' gi'e [give] their happy souls, drough [through] greace,
> A higher pleace than Herrenston.

Now if we consider these words and thoughts in the context of Barnes' life and philosophy, then what he is saying is quite remarkable. We know that Barnes was himself of the people, whose speech and folklore he admired and described both in poetry and in learned articles. It might therefore have seemed curious that he should write of the 'Saxon's' (i.e. English countryman's) destructiveness, and how he needed a refining example from above. In fact we can only understand this seeming paradox if we take into account his linguistic views which we shall describe in detail in Part Two of this book. For Barnes' fundamental intuition was that the English language suffered from the fact that all its learned vocabulary concerning for example, administration, government, military affairs, technology, was Norman-French or Latin in origin. The learned 'Saxon' compounds of English had virtually all been lost with the Norman Conquest. As he had written as long ago as 1832: 'The English are a great nation; and as an Englishman, I am sorry that we have not a language of our own; but that whenever we happen to conceive a thought above that of a plough-boy, or produce anything beyond a pitch-fork, we are obliged to borrow a word from others before we can utter it, or give it a name'.[101] But just as England had lost an elite language with the Norman Conquest, so it had also lost its social elite.

In wishing for an enlightened squirearchy, what Barnes really wanted was the restoration of the patriarchal 'atheldom' or nobility of Saxon 'folk' England – that which had perished at the Battle of Hastings, or been dispossessed by Norman warrior and fled into exile abroad. The promotion of a governing class, sympathetic to the poor, was certainly part of Barnes' message given in his constant lecturing in the West Country. Indeed this is even one of the fruits of Barnes' dialect poetry, as one sympathetic reviewer wrote: 'This, we would trust, may be among the consequences of the present publication, to keep alive, in some measure, the interest in the affairs of the Poor... If the Landlords and upper classes generally may thus be led to a more intimate acquaintance with the feelings and habits (of the poor) and to a more sincere sympathy with their wants, and hopes, and fears; if they may be taught in any degree to have a respect for their homely and household prejudices which are far too frequently violated and despised, we are convinced that Mr. Barnes will feel that his poems have aided in a work whose success he would value far above any fame or emolument that may accrue to himself... All the poor want is to be known and to be communicated with directly... instead of being left to the tender mercies of an ill-educated class, whose own bargains have been often hardly driven, and whose prosperity, therefore, depends upon oppression and illiberality. Against this treatment their only weapon is deceit; and the consciousness of deceiving produces a savage gloom in their character and a suspiciousness of the upper classes'.[102]

In other words what Barnes was seeking in an enlightened squirearchy was none other than the restoration of a social system which had

---

[101] 'On Compounds in the English Language', *Gentleman's Magazine* 1832, Supplementary Volume CII, p.593
[102] Quoted in Hearl, pp.180-1

certainly been greatly shaken, though not altogether destroyed, with the imposition of a foreign and unsympathetic ruling class onto it centuries before. This is why he could write of the need for a refining influence on 'the Saxon mind'; Saxon England had lost not only the learned compounds used by its elite, but also, through massacre, exile or dispossession, the elite itself. Since then the relation between landed and landless, rich and poor had been unsteady, divisive, first on account differences of race and language between English and Norman, then on account of the differences of class and culture. Wittingly or unwittingly, Barnes was promoting in both his poetry and prose works not only the speech of rural, pre-industrial England, which harked back to the speech of Saxon, pre-Conquest England, but also the social attitudes, structures, patterns of thought and expectations of rural, pre-industrial England, which ultimately harked back to those of Saxon, pre-Conquest England. What at heart Barnes wanted to see was the restoration of the paternalism of the Saxon hall and church, whose descendants he instinctively, though probably at first unconsciously, saw in the enlightened nineteenth century squire and 'parson'. The images and even words of his poem 'Herrenston, 'Vor me'th, avore their roaren vier, An' roun' their bwoard, 'ithin the hall', describe not so much a nineteenth century Dorset village feast as the festive board of a paternal, patriarchal, protective Saxon lord as he made feast with his folk. Barnes wanted the gentlefolk of England to be Christian and cultured, to be with the people, and to use their positions and wealth in charity towards their fellows. Elsewhere in an Eclogue, 'The Times', he wrote:

> If we've a-got a friend at all,
> Why who can tell -I'm sure thou cassen [canst not] –
> But that the squier, or the pa'son,
> Mid [Might] be our friend, Tom, after all?

Barnes' vision was that of the rural community of the paternal and therefore respected Saxon lord and lady with his hall and Saxon priest with his church, which had officially disappeared with the imposition of Norman feudalism and the Norman Church, a foreign Establishment elite. At first unconsciously as a village boy, later consciously as a linguist, Anglo-Saxonist, antiquarian, teacher, polymath and polyglot, he preached the restoration of this social ideal of Saxon England, transposed into his own age, into the community of the enlightened squire and the country rector.

Thus the seemingly backwards-looking traditionalism of William Barnes was in fact a radical and revolutionary social philosophy, which challenged the ultimately Norman-English class conflict of English society and called for the governing class to overcome it. And this relevance for the present should hardly surprise us, who have witnessed the tragic consequences of class divisions in English society into Establishment and People, Management and Unions, 'them and us', especially in recent years. At a time when large corporations all revere the ideas of teamwork, quality circles, total quality and the importance of social responsibility, at a time when Taylorism is dead and management gurus predict 'flat' companies without hierarchies thanks to the triumph of the 'knowledge worker', at a time when politicians of left and right talk freely of 'communitarianism' and the 'social market', how can we not find Barnes' insights relevant?

And if we are surprised by the relevance of Barnes' social vision, then we can do no better than read once more the words of Barnes' daughter in her biography of her beloved father: 'Some men live before their age, others behind it. My father did both. in action he was behind the world, or rather apart from it; in thought he was far before his time... A great and deep student of the past, he drew from it inferences and teaching for the future'.[103]

---

[103] Baxter, Preface

Chapter 6

Economics

It is often said that the interests of capital and labour are identical, and so in truth they are as long as they are kept so by the law of Christian kindness.

William Barnes, *Views of Labour and Gold*, p.70.

One of the great problems of the twentieth century has undoubtedly been the conflict between capital and labour, a conflict which had appeared already in the industrialised countries of the nineteenth century. It is precisely the conflict that arises with industrialisation, causing so much strife between workers and owners and giving rise to conflicting ideologies and even actual wars, such as those that have taken place between Marxist Communism and Western Capitalism. Prophetically, above all in his work of 1859 *Views of Labour and Gold*, as a forerunner from the past, William Barnes foresaw these struggles: '...in a community of rich idlers, care should be taken of the honest working classes, or else they will become degraded and dangerous'.[104] Tragically, it would seem that we are able to appreciate his wisdom only at the end of the twentieth century and all its bitter experience. Let us now look specifically at what he had to say on the questions of labour and capital- starting with labour.

First of all, Barnes says that work is necessary for man. In this he reiterates the Christian view taken from Genesis where as a result of the cosmic catastrophe of the Fall, Paradise is lost and fallen Adam in future has to make a living by the sweat of his brow. However, not all work, thinks Barnes, is good for man and he states quite openly: '...there is reason to believe that the most healthy modes of winning a livelihood were the earliest ones of hunting, herdsmanship and free tillage, in which there was a good action, without too long a toil, of the lungs and of all the limbs

---

[104] *VLG* p.163

of the body in the open air'.[105] This again related to Genesis – the curse of Adam was precisely to work the land, not to work in a machine-shop. Barnes goes on to cite examples of many peoples in the world renowned for their good health and comeliness on account of working in the fresh air, ending on a typically humorous note with the instance, recorded some sixty years before, of girls at Newport on the Isle of Wight, 'lovely and elegantly dressed'... 'Whether these fair maids have transmitted their charms to the present blooming daughters of the island farms I know not, and it is a question the solution of which may be perilous for a bachelor to undertake'.[106] Barnes also praises the virtues of gardening both for physical exercise and for economic reasons, to grow food, and he was clearly a firm supporter of the allotment system.[107]

This is not to say, however, that he was in favour of physical work alone: 'Man is a being of body and soul. The hand labourers [manual workers) of a community work for the body, and their occupation, while it gives them an admirable craft of hand, tends only to keep the soul, untrained in its true life of purity and intelligence, still dark and dull'.[108] For this reason Barnes finds needful the existence of a class to administrate, clergy, lawyers, teachers (like himself), an army etc. This is the only justification that he finds for the institution of servants, 'to take lower work from their employers, and so to set their hands and minds free for work of higher kinds... So the free time which is gained by the service of others in lower work is not afforded for idle pleasure, but for good work of a higher kind'.[109]

What Barnes finds harmful, as we have already mentioned in the previous chapter, is the existence of a class, who, while not toiling with their hands, produce nothing in other ways either, in other

---

[105] op. cit., pp.120-1
[106] op. cit., p.124
[107] op. cit., pp.125-6. These views were first expressed as early as 1829, when Barnes put them in a letter to the Dorset County Chronicle.
[108] *VLG* p.172. These views also appear earlier in 'Humilis Domus', in the *Poole and Dorset Herald* (PDH) 3/5/1849.
[109] *VLG* p.117

words, the rich and idle. Here Barnes is completely logical: since he accepts that the sons of Adam must work, whatever form that work may take, he cannot accept idleness: 'The increase of a truly idle class, a class who may do nothing for the bodily man, and cannot work any good to the intellectual one, is a social evil'.[110] And of the working but idle man, he whom today we would call unemployed, he says: 'The reaction of inaction on the mind and body, is hardly less harmful than that of the worst kinds of action... Inaction of body tends to breed weakness...'.[111]

On the other hand Barnes totally rejects overwork. In an unbalanced society, with idle rich, others are forced to overwork. The overworked man 'has no time to solace himself with the gifts of his God... no time to enlighten and purify his soul by a peaceful reading of the word of life... While moderate labour is wholesome to the body and good to the mind, excessive daily toil is fraught with evil to the body and soul... Man goeth forth to his work until the evening, the word of God tells us; but the life of the overworked man in some parts of England almost belies it... A day's toil should be sweetened by the foretaste of the evening of freedom that looms from beyond it; and the week's labour should be like a walk through the nave of a cathedral, bright from the light at the end of it... Let the poor, therefore, have some time, if it can be anyhow afforded them, to seek light for their own minds and grace for their own hearts...'.[112] In his Eclogue, 'Father Come Hwome' he shows that the result of the Enclosures, poverty, not only means physical deprivation, but lack of time and energy to cultivate oneself. Self-improvement is not possible amid overwork and the resulting exhaustion. This, though most moderately expressed, is in fact a sweeping denunciation, revolutionary beyond Marx, of all the horrors of the Industrial Age, so prominent in Barnes' nineteenth century England.

---

[110] op. cit. p.173
[111] op. cit. p.89
[112] 'Humilis Domus', *PDH* 26/4/1849

Indeed, if we may sum up these views, we come to some very radical results indeed: William Barnes wanted a society in which everyone, including the rich, worked, nobody was idle in unemployment, but nobody was overworked. And since he saw man as a unity of body, soul and mind, he considered that man should also be able to cultivate all the aspects of his being. Thus the labourer, in field or factory, should be allowed to cultivate mind and soul and have time to spend with his family. For this end he even suggested that the working man should have one half-day free every week. And the 'mind-worker' should not forget physical work, he could, for example, exercise himself through gardening. The society envisioned by Barnes is in many ways the *opposite* of that in which we live and he lived. Though today many, but by no means all, have an eight-hour day and a free weekend, Barnes' vision of social justice has never in fact been implemented. Now if we are to look at how Barnes envisioned the uses of 'gold' in the form of nineteenth century capitalism, we shall even further appreciate just how radical his views were.

The fact that capitalism led to overwork was caused, felt Barnes, by excessive competition: 'If all tradesmen could restrain the tyranny of competition, and close the eyelids of their shops in earlier rest, none would lose money by it... If all shops were closed an hour earlier, late buyers would be earlier ones by an hour'.[113] Such a fundamental criticism presuppose that people are capable of restraining their greed – a presupposition of social and personal values permeated by Christian values. As if to add insult to the capitalist ethic he had already injured, Barnes then goes on to decry mechanisation – the whole basis of the Machine Age: 'Machinery transfers rather than lessens labour... in truth, machines tend to derange the labour market... since the men displaced from their work by the machine are not at once qualified by skill to go back to the other end of the labour, and make the machine that is to do the work from which their hands have been displaced'.[114] Now is this not the cry of despair of the

---

[113] *VLG* p.89
[114] *VLG* p.107

unskilled worker of the 1990s who has been replaced by the computer and the robot?

Today we may not agree with Barnes that machines transfer rather than lessen labour, but if we put ourselves into the nineteenth century context, perhaps we would agree with Barnes when he says: 'I want to see, but cannot find, that machinery lessens labour, and that it lessens it so far that it sends home the labourer to his wife and children and his garden, or rest, and book, and friendly talk, an hour earlier in the evening, and until I see this happy effect of it, I cannot welcome it as a great good... machinery has drawn into its grasp the bodies of young children...'.[115] The nineteenth century was, after all, a period when twelve- and fourteen-hour days for men, women and children alike were all too frequent. And Barnes was only too aware of the exploitation, especially of children, in the nineteenth century. Giving evidence to the Royal Commission on the Employment of Children, Young Persons and Women, he later declared that many rural families were dependent on the pennies their children could earn – indeed, some employers would only employ a father if he were also able to exploit the son, paying him a pittance.[116]

Moreover, adds Barnes, a machine cannot reproduce the quality of the hand-made article, nor does it have a good effect on body or mind: 'There is machinery which holds the labourer in unwholesome places, and under unwholesome agencies, with too great a sameness of action and posture, and has to answer for a good share of torn limbs, broken bones, and untimely deaths...'.[117] Now this is clearly an argument against one of the most fundamental concepts and realities of the whole Industrial Age – the division of labour, and Barnes does not beat about the bush – like his contemporaries, Carlyle, Ruskin and late Morris, he is largely against it: 'I believe that excessive division of labour is most pernicious to the workman's health and to his perfection as a man'.[118]

---

[115] op. cit.
[116] Written Evidence given in the Commission's 'Blue Book'. Appendix Part II to the second report, pp.12-1414 *VLG* p.111.
[117] *VLG* p.111
[118] op. cit., p.3

He finds that repetitive tasks can be dangerous for the health, thus a needle grinder eventually dies of breathing steel dust all day and every day, the glassblower and the miner die hasty deaths and a woman who works all day at a loom may do her job well but will be incapable of doing anything else.[119] In the same way parts of the body become atrophied because they are not used on account of the division of labour whereby the worker performs only one repetitive task. This is the denunciation of the production-line, of 'Fordism' and 'Taylorism', before Ford and Taylor were even born, and it tallies with many of the ideas about the quality of working life that companies have tried to implement in the last generation.

Barnes opposed the results of the division of labour – factory-made goods: 'When I was a little chap if I wanted a top or a whistle I must make it; but now ever so smart a one can be bought for a half-penny... but you can't take pride in a thing which you didn't make'.[120] Here we are on the same ground as William Morris who later wrote: 'Time was when everyone that made anything, made a work of art besides a useful piece of goods; and it gave them pleasure to do it'. Barnes also opposed the 'congregation of labour', caused by its division, where, 'its throng of labourers are sometimes excited by sudden fits of crowd-moodiness to acts of violence, or a behaviour of defiance'. The result says Barnes, is 'the conspiracy of strikes' which are then put down 'by the soldier's sword or policeman's bludgeon'.[121] This must be familiar to all of us who have lived in the England of the 1980s. He adds, moreover: 'We can hardly believe that congregated labour can be overwhelmingly needful, since it is not found congregated in all lands in such cases as it holds with us'.[122] Now Barnes wrote these words well over 100 years before Schumacher wrote the best-selling ever book on Economics, 'Small is Beautiful'. Barnes' vision of the Economy was that of the cottage economy.

---

[119] op. cit., pp.3-5
[120] Baxter, p.203
[121] *VLG* p.114
[122] op. cit., p.115

Having denounced jobs which have unwelcome physical and social effects, Barnes goes on to denounce those which should simply not be performed at all: 'We ought not to overlook those (kinds of labour) which may have a bad reaction on the conscience; and which, however easy may be their action, and however great may be their gain, are not to be earnestly chosen by Christian men; since, as they deaden the conscience, they likewise do harm to the soul'.[123] Into this category Barnes puts the gambling-house, the house of ill-fame, criminal activities, the adulteration of food (by artificial colourings and flavourings – or feeding herbivorous cows contaminated sheep carcasses?), businesses where lying and deception are involved, and the tasks of the hangman and the slave-trader. 'The labour of the swindler, thief and forger, the over-reacher, and the adulterator of food, may be slight and well-paid in money; but the reaction, if not on the body in the way of punishment, yet on the soul in the way of fear, or uneasiness, or the warping of the judgement, and the blunting of the conscience, and the ill-will of men, and guilt with God, is such as to leave a vast balance of evil rather than of good in the wealth of sinful toil'.[124] Ironically, Barnes finds that, 'callings or labours of least service to man's true welfare, are not unfrequently best rewarded by worldly gain... The selling of one's conscience to powers of evil win worldly rewards more readily than a standing by the truth against sin... In short, cunning and selfishness, and unrighteousness of several kinds, may bring in more ready money than goodness and truth'.[125] Such views, if systematically and conscientiously put into practice, would have utterly transformed the society of Barnes' time, let alone our own.

These deformations of working practice, the excessive division of labour, overwork, the idle rich, the tyranny of the machine, unhealthy working conditions, the growth of soul-destroying tasks and activities, were ultimately for Barnes all part of the same movement towards Mammon-worship which was running through England and

---

[123] op. cit., pp.33-4
[124] op. cit., p.93
[125] op. cit., p.118

he sternly denounced the temptations and abuses of capital: 'The reaction of sudden riches on a mind unhallowed and untrained for the stewardship of them is in many cases most pernicious... whether our newly-awakened yearnings (from suddenly-received riches) would be good or evil, spiritual or sensual, for noble or grovelling aims, would arise from our fullness or lack of the better gifts of grace... One bad reaction of wealth upon some minds is arrogance or purse pride... Another reaction of wealth may be greediness and the hoarding mind of the miser'.[126] Miserliness, says Barnes, is a blindness to the natural beauty of the world, nay, to life itself: 'Another feeling allied to that of miserliness is the money-making mind, which looks on the works of God or the pursuits of man mainly, if not only, as sources of wealth, and on the promotion of trade as an end that is well gained over every other good. Such a mind may look on time only as a form of space for the doing of business; on education only as a qualification for gainful employments; on a handsome tree only as the loss or gain upon a balance of the commercial value of its yearly growth, and the yield of the ground it takes up; on a waterfall only as a power for an overshot wheel'.[127] Such comments, denouncing the 'Time is Money' mentality may also remind us of the sad fate of certain National Lottery winners in our own times.

Nevertheless, despite these denunciations, we should not imagine that Barnes was against material wealth as such. He was rather against its abuse, in accordance with the much misquoted Pauline teaching, not that money is the root of all evil, but that '*the love of money* is the root of all evil' (I Tim.6,10). 'I may spend capital on labour worthy of an angel, or the labour of demons... A landowner may bestow his capital on the improvement of his estate, and the houses, and sheds, and roads, and bridges of his people, or he may lay it out in a ship and tackle for the slave trade. In the former case it becomes at once an agency of good, and in the other it is an agency of evil; and so it either increases or diminishes the sum of happiness'.[128] Barnes

---

[126] op. cit., p.118
[127] op. cit., p.57
[128] op. cit., p.119

constantly denounced what he called 'tradesmanship' [commercialism] – a denunciation which must have cost his school dear in terms of the tradesmen's sons lost to it: 'It would bring us no harm if the up-growing generation of this 'Nation of Shopkeepers' could be brought to feel that there is a source of purer happiness than even that of converting fourpenny pieces into sixpences. The end of wealth-getting must be happiness, but we think that the wearisome toils of the wealth-winner are not always the shortest way to it. The naturalist, wandering among his summer blossoms or glittering insects, or the poet or painter, with his heart leaping at the glories of God's earth, may have found it at much less cost of gold'.[129] Now this is a viewpoint which no politician in this country has ever dared express. Another denunciation challenges many of the assumptions of recent years, as he condemns the situation whereby, 'a cunning and successful trader in the shares of swindling companies may be as much esteemed as a farmer, or builder, or weaver, or tanner'.[130] And he sums up his attitude to the rich who can afford all manner of costly luxuries and are sycophantically honoured by society by saying: 'Let us not withhold honour from the man who can afford to keep a conscience which, if we reckon the worldly gain that must be foregone to hold the most precious treasure, is of the greatest cost'.[131] In this case, as is so often the case with Barnes these views are taken directly from the Gospel: 'For where your treasure is, there will your heart be also' (Matt. 6,21). 'The selling of one's conscience to powers of evil wins worldly rewards more readily than a standing by the truth against sin... In short, cunning and selfishness, and unrighteousness of several kinds, may bring in more ready money than goodness and truth'.[132] Commenting on the new mentality, Barnes wrote in his poem 'The Leane': 'What's zwold [sold] an' bought Is all that is worthy o' thought!

---

[129] *Gentleman's Magazine*, October 1848, pp.397-9
[130] *VLG* p.101
[131] op. cit., pp.118-9
[132] op. cit., p.118

If the passion for riches through trade is extended to the international arena, then the consequences, from Barnes' viewpoint, are perhaps even more horrifying: 'The money-making mind... looks on the discovery of a new land only as that of new resources of trade; on a newly reached people only as buyers of our wares; and on a war on a people who have never lifted a hand against us, otherwise than as meddlers with their own laws and towns, as a fine opening up of a trade'.[133] Topically, for the period when he was writing, he quotes a writer from Canton as saying: 'I should say the Chinese lost about a thousand killed during the bombardment and attack. If this loss of life is weighed against the increased prosperity that will, without doubt, be seen and felt in the city after a short period of the rule of the Western Powers, I think the most prejudiced must admit that the course taken has been the most humane'. Barnes concludes that the logic of the writer is: 'If we can improve the prosperity of a town by shooting a share of its inhabitants, it is humane to shoot them'.[134]

Barnes' denunciation is a no more and no less than a denunciation of the *whole history* of Western Imperialism, from the Crusades on to South and North America, Africa, Asia and Australasia, wherever Western peoples carried out genocides on native inhabitants in the name of filthy lucre – and he was an Anglican priest of the middle of the nineteenth century! Can we possibly still think of Barnes as a 'conformist', a 'yes-man' (as E. M. Forster so mistakenly called him)? Of the evil of the Opium Wars Barnes wrote that since the Chinese had no need to trade, the British had forced them into trading by creating a need, the need to buy opium – a poison. He said further: 'With nations, a state wins more land and wealth by sending the sword against weak tribes than affording them missionaries or other good teachers; and we may be gaining money faster by selling the Chinese opium... than we should by taking to them the most wholesome kinds of food'.[135] Moreover, Barnes foresaw the international dangers of 'tradesmanship', those very dangers which

---

[133] op. cit., pp.57-8
[134] op. cit.
[135] op. cit., p.118

were to lead directly to the horrors of the First World War. The same government that 'supported fighting 'traders' quarrels in China and Japan, was also that which 'cringed to powerful states, as we do not now even dare to tell Prussia and Austria of their wrongs to their faces'.[136] There is no doubt that, as just he opposed 'tradesmanship' and its division of labour inside Great Britain, he certainly opposed Free Trade, which favoured only the strong and the rich, those who already started off with some 'comparative advantage', and not the farmer, the rural backbone of the land, who could only sell produce without added value.[137] Barnes was certainly a protectionist, for he wanted to protect the rural way of life: 'Zoo now mid nwone [might none] ov us vorget The pattern our vorefathers zet' (From his poem, 'Our Fathers' Works').

At the end of this survey of William Barnes' economic views, it is the writer's hope that the reader will have been stimulated by the radical and often highly topical tenor of Barnes' thought. Of commentators, we have found only one who seems to have realised the importance of Barnes' thought on political economy, Rev. O. P. Cambridge, one of Barnes' many outstanding pupils, who foresaw the day when profit-sharing would come to exist – thanks in part to Barnes' thought. Writing his 'In Memoriam' in 1887, he commented: '…the relations of labour and capital are discussed thus earnestly and temperately. If space allowed we might show how fair he (Barnes) is to capital rightly employed, and how dear to his heart were the interests and well-being of the working man… But what I consider the essential point in this work is the insistence upon a higher law than the law of the land, and the market price as a factor in the relations of labour and capital – 'the law of Christian Kindness'…Mr. Barnes was not merely a poet… but a true, a large-hearted and just philanthropist; and I venture to think that Mr. Barnes' fame will not in the future simply rest upon his Dorset Dialect poems…'.[138]

---

[136] Baxter, p.333
[137] Hearl, pp.162-3
[138] 'In Memoriam' Rev. William Barnes, *Proceedings of the Dorset Natural History and Archaeological Society*, Vol. VIII (1887), p.xxv

It is then our thought that much of what Barnes reflected on and wrote of is prophetic. He has lessons for us today. In our post-Keynesian but also post-Thatcherite society, his pre-industrial views may have relevance for us: 'Barnes was something of a radical 'Little Englander' – and in keeping with such a viewpoint he was suspicious of State intervention... He was opposed to expansionary capitalism, the desire for trade at any cost... the concept of labour as nothing more than a factor in production... calling only in this society for a redistribution of resources from the idle to the worthy poor. He did not urge more and more work to create more and more wealth. His ideal was not wealth but to be like the uncle in the title of his poem 'Uncle Out O' Debt An' Out O' Danger'. Barnes felt that the right amount of labour by people was that which earned them adequate food, clothing and shelter 'without pernicious luxuries' or items 'needless otherwise than to pride or vice, or which supplied the means of existence for classes unworking in any way for the community'.[139] Such words may strike a chord in societies where State intervention has been largely discredited, but where also the social injustices of unchecked deregulation and inhuman profiteering have cast into doubt the free market ideas of economic liberalism.

By many contemporary economists Barnes might be called a 'populist'. And in the sense that Barnes never lost his roots, as is symbolised by his love of the Dorset dialect, indeed he was a populist. He was for the country people, the 'Saxon landfolk' as he called them, he was for the underdog, tirelessly working into his old age to spread knowledge among the working people of the South-West. On the other hand, as we shall see in the next chapter, he was no party political man and disliked any sort of political organisation. In Economics, Barnes sought not wealth but goodness, he possessed that unique and most revolutionary wisdom to value what is beyond price – a clear conscience: the aim of work was 'to work righteously with a hope of winning daily bread' and no more.[140] 'There are three

---

[139] Chris Wrigley, 'William Barnes and the Social Problem', *Dorset Natural History and Archaeological Society, Proceedings for 1977*, p.26
[140] *VLG* p.119

divine gifts which are the elements of true happiness or wealth; the spiritual one of righteousness; the bodily one of health; and the social one of good government; but the more common kinds of worldly wealth are of uncertain effect, though the peace of a community is none the safer for a greater inequality of wealth, such that one class may be over-rich to wanton luxury, while another are poor to naked hunger'.[141] And in a poem, 'The Ivy', he wrote:

> Oh! why do vo'k so often chaïn
> Their pinen minds vor love o' gaïn,
> An' gi'e their innocence to rise
> A little in the worold's eyes?
> If pride could lift us to the skies,
> What man do value, God do slight,
> An' all is nothen in His zight
> 'Ithout an honest heart, John.

Barnes' economic views were human, taking into account conventional economic facts, they also took into account the spiritual wealth of righteousness. 'The wordle don't ax [ask] what A body [somebody] is, but only what he's got' were the words he wrote in his Eclogue 'The New Poor Laws'. This was his critique of Capitalist Society, a society based only on money. His views were shaped by the Gospel and rooted in the life of the 'Saxon' people who worked the land, his views were human and divine at one and the same time – in that sense they may be called 'Saxon Economics'.

To those who would have remained unsatisfied with this view because it failed to involve itself in party politics, Barnes replied. In his poem 'Zickness', he wrote:

> An' bags o' money at the end o' time
> Can't buy a soul, nor meäke amends vor crime.
> The men wi' wealth mus' lose it at their death,
> The poor do gi'e up little but their breath'.

---

[141] op. cit., p.53

And in his poem *Withstanders* (the Resisters), we are given a vision of the world to come, where might is not right, the wicked do not prosper and all the wronged are righted before the Saviour and righteous humanity stands bodily in the transfigured ('starbright') glory of Him Who is the Source of Ultimate Social and Economic Justice:

> When weakness now do strive wi' might
> In struggles ov an e'thly trial, Might mid overcome the right,
> An' truth be turn'd by might's denial...
> But when the wicked, now so strong,
> Shall stan' vor judgement, peäle as ashes,
> By the souls that rued their wrong,
> Wi' tears a-hangen on their lashes...
> Sweet children o' the dead, bereft
> Ov all their goods by guile an' forgen;
> Souls o'driven sleaves that left
> Their weary limbs a-mark'd by scourgen...
> The maid that selfish craft led on
> To sin, an' left wi' hope a-blighted;
> Starvèn workmen, thin an' wan,
> Wi' hopeless leabour ill requited;
> Souls a-wrong'd, an call'd to vill
> Wi' dread, the man that us'd em [used them] ill.
> When might shall yield to right as pliant,
> As a dwarf avore a giant.
> When there, at last, the good shall glow
> In starbright bodies lik' their Seäviour,
> Vor all their flesh noo mwore mid show
> The marks o' man's unkind beheäviour:
> Wi' speechless tongue, an burnen cheäk,
> The strong shall bow avore the weäk,
> An' vind that helplessness, wi' right,
> Is strong beyond all e'thly might.

Chapter 7

Politics

For what is England that she should be dear to me, but that she is the land that owns my county? Why should I love my county, but that it contains the village of my birth? Why should that village be hallowed in my mind, but that it holds the home of my childhood?

William Barnes, 'Humilis Domus'

Imperialism is a depraved choice of national life, imposed by self-seeking interests which appeal to the lusts of quantitative acquisitiveness and of forceful domination surviving in a nation from early centuries of animal struggle for existence. Its adoption as a policy implies a deliberate renunciation of that cultivation of the higher inner qualities which for a nation as for an individual constitutes the ascendancy of reason over brute impulse. It is the besetting sin of all successful States, and its penalty is unalterable in the order of nature.

J. A. Hobson, *Imperialism a Study*, 1902

Since political views are in so many ways a synthesis of social and economic views, this last chapter of Part One of this work will form a summary of the previous two chapters and to some extent of the whole of Part One.

It might perhaps seem strange to talk of the political views of Rev. William Barnes, for he did not like political parties, never belonged to one, and it would be pointless to comb through his writings in search of some directly political comment or an indication of how he may have voted at elections. Barnes disliked both power and money – the two main preoccupations of politics and politicians, and he called himself a 'political heretic'. Indeed he spent a part of his life hovering on the edge of poverty and seems to have been despised by the local Dorchester Establishment for his selfless lack of ambition. On the other hand, there are many implications or comments in his works which have indirect bearings on Barnes' political orientations. Let us first, however, try to uncover Barnes' attitude to his own country, then the most powerful in the world, and its actions and influence outside its own borders.

Firstly it is quite clear that Barnes disliked Imperialism – a policy pursued by both the political parties of his day. This is clear as early as 1849 when he spoke forthrightly against the occupation of the lands of other peoples, justified by some by the Biblical text that man should multiply and replenish the earth: 'We are fearful that the logic by which we take the lands of others under this authority, is not perfectly sound. The truth is that the red men of America, and the darker ones of Australia and New Zealand, are children of Adam, and therefore *they* are bidden with *us* to replenish the earth, and are fulfilling the injunction till we go and stop them, by the occupation of the lands over which they might be spreading'.[142] What Barnes is saying is astoundingly modern, for he is saying that all men are sons of Adam, not just Western Europeans. In so doing he unmasks the deeply unpleasant racist arrogance of those who justified Imperialism which was implicit in their whole ideology, which asserted that Western man and culture were inherently superior to all others and that the 'coloured savages' of the Americas, Africa, Asia and Australasia were really no better than animals since they were not really human. He criticises the idea that Christians, simply because they were Christians, had the inherent right to seize the lands of non-Christians: '…as if Christians could draw from the positive precept, the new commandment of their Divine Saviour 'to love one another', the negative one that they might plunder all men not yet within the fold of the Church. It is to be feared that as a nation, we have to answer for much unrighteousness towards weaker tribes'.[143]

With these few, seemingly moderate words, Barnes denounces the whole, many-centuried process of Empire-building, beginning with the Crusades, which Western Powers justified through their

---

[142] 'Humilis Domus', *Poole and Dorset Herald* (PDH), 24/5/1849
[143] op. cit.

distortions of the Christian Faith. In his 'Views of Labour and Gold', as we have already mentioned, Barnes had condemned the Opium Wars and Western Imperialism in China. Of the West Indies he spoke of a writer who justifying the sugar and rum trade, 'has stated, seemingly without any misgivings of conscience, that he himself had worked slaves eighteen hours a day at cropping time'.[144] Barnes' views on slavery were quite clear; he considered it to be as destructive to its masters as to the slaves. Perhaps, however, the clearest and most extraordinary (for the period) denunciation of the Imperialist mentality came two years before the publication of 'Views of Labour and Gold', when on seventh October 1857 he preached in Dorchester's main church – no doubt in front of the town's social elite. This was the Day of Humiliation, the Day of National Mourning for those massacred in the Indian Mutiny. Since it is such an important statement of Barnes' position, we shall quote from it at some length:

'Was this day of humiliation to own ourselves as sinful as a nation, and yet not to try our behaviour by the pattern of the mind that is in Christ? What is the high place to which we as a nation have been too often going for ages? Dominion. Land. Gold. In one word: Mammon... the first danger is pride. The tokens of our pride are seen in our writings in which we see Englishmen arrogantly boasting of England's might instead of yearning with fear for her godly use of it. Another danger is injustice, or when dominion or wealth can be won with ease, a selfish readiness to mistake the opportunity of taking it for God's call to it; and justify our taking it by worldly maxims, instead of the law of Christ... Look at the power we hold in India, and the evil that has notwithstanding arisen against us... There is a doctrine which is nevertheless a dangerous one. It is that the Lord of the Earth has given to us, the English nation, a wide dominion, so that inasmuch as we hold a pure form of faith our sword may make way for the Gospel... Has no Englishman, standing proudly on the power of England, behaved among men

---

[144] *Views of Labour and Gold (VLG)*, p.58

of another religion as if our own had been wanting in the power of hallowing his heart? If we are guilty in these cases, how will it help us that we have a pure form of Faith? We want pure hearts, pure lives... One of the un-Christian maxims so common among us is often taken up not only against weaker tribes, but against men of a lower status of life – that they cannot appreciate kindness, but mistake it for weakness, and therefore we cannot be too severe, too cruel with them. It is a Satanic argument to reconcile the conscience to injustice and cruelty... Missionary work will never be done by the sword, the sceptre, nor the civil power of itself. They may make thousands of hypocrites, but no conversions. Conversion must be the work of the word and the spirit... Let us be sure we do our missionary work with a missionary spirit, and that if we strive for the conversion of the heathen it is for their good, and not for our gain in a freer and easier form of trade. They who have taken the sword will perish by the sword. There was no need for our Saviour to take the form of man to teach him to avenge his wrongs. the worst of men did it before the Incarnation... My work is peace and salvation... Remember as a warning that though a people may gain in dominion, in population, in land, in wealth by a sinful act, they are by that act weaker than they were before it'.[145]

Thus Barnes condemned the ethnocentric arrogance of the Western Powers to other cultures, which in fact was a mere camouflage for lust for power, land and gold, and which had existed 'for ages', as he said in this sermon.

The arrogance condemned here was arrogance to others who lived in the same historical era. He also, however, condemned the arrogance of the West towards its own past, implicit in its belief in progress. In his 'Notes on Ancient Britain and the Britons', written in 1858, he wrote: 'Some of our school-books tell their readers that the Britons

---

[145] Sermon on the Day of Humiliation, p.39, Scrapbook 2 in the Dorset County Museum Barnes Archive.

wore the skins of beasts, as it were a token of great misery; but... a fur coat is no token of misery... in an English railway carriage through a snowy day!'.[146] Combining criticisms of attitudes to both the past and to other cultures he wrote that the Ancient Egyptians, 'were a nation learned in the sciences when the inhabitants of Europe were wild in the woods, and... the Hindoos applied a system of fluxions of their own to the quadrature of the circle before Sir Isaac Newton or Leibnitz was born'.[147]

Barnes' denunciation of arrogance, both in time (towards past history) and space (towards contemporary peoples and cultures) would most certainly have alienated him from the Imperialist wings of the Tory Party and also the Liberal Whig Party of his day which found that Imperial trade justified colonial aggression and war (the Crimean War, the Opium Wars, the Balkan Wars of Muslim Turkey with their horrific massacres of Balkan Christians, and later, it must be said, the Boer War and the First World War). On the other hand, and this may at first seem paradoxical, Barnes, as a patriot and an Anglican priest who disliked Non-Conformism, and wrote against the Disestablishment of the Church of England, both of which he thought weakened the unity of Church and Nation, was therefore in some way a member of the Establishment, an antidisestablishmentarian. How can this seeming contradiction be accounted for? I think that if we define Barnes' patriotism, then we shall understand that there is no contradiction in reality.

Barnes' patriotism was in fact local, it was home-love, England held 'the home of his childhood', as we have quoted above. He loved the place where he had met God in his blissful childhood. And that childhood had not been spent in the slumdom of Manchester or London but in the virtually untouched, millennial Dorset countryside. This was a regular theme in his poetry. In 'Praise O' Do'set', he wrote:

---

[146] *Notes on Ancient Britain and the Britons*, p.13
[147] Education in Words and in Things, *Gentleman's Magazine* January, p.22

We Do'set, though we mid [might] be hwomely,
Ben't [Aren't] asheam'd to own our pleace...
Friend an' wife,
Fathers, mothers, sisters, brothers,
Happy, happy be their life!
Vor Do'set dear,
Then gi'e woone cheer;
D'ye hear? woone cheer!

And in 'The Girt Woak Tree That's In The Dell' he described how he would fight for his country, but standing on ship's planks made from the favourite oak tree of his childhood:

An' I upon his planks would stand,
An' die a-fighten vor the land,-
The land so dear,-the land so dear,-the land so free,-
The land that bore the girt woak tree.

Barnes then was a local patriot, a 'home-lover': 'It is to the house that we must look for the growth of many of the most lovely social Christian graces: the affections of kindred, a reverence for the kindly feelings, and a love of home, which in its full outgrowth, becomes that bulwark of the safety of a community and constitution, 'amor patriae', the love of one's fatherland'.[148] He was also a highly cultured and intelligent man. He was in no way a nationalistic 'patriot', a jingoist, an attitude which at the time must have cost him dear, in part certainly the rejection of the social elite of Dorset. Thus to call Barnes a 'Little Englander', though an anachronism since the expression dates from 1890, would seem to us the most exact definition of his position. He was a local patriot, one who loved only the beauty and good and truth in the England he knew – and not the soul destroying Mammon-worship of tradesmanship, of Victorian industrialism with its ragged, urban proletariat, worker exploitation, colonial rape and all its hypocritical justifications for its sins..

---

[148] *VLG* p.170

The closest Barnes ever came to a political statement was in his Eclogue 'The Times', where he wrote against the Chartists – 'the socialists of those days'. Here his character John (bearing the same name as Barnes' commonsense yeoman father) speaks against Tom: 'Ah! I do think you mid as well be quiet; You'll meäke things wo'se, i'-ma'-be [it maybe], by a riot'. Barnes considered that the intervention of the townee Chartist would make the situation of the farm-labourer even worse than before. However he later regretted these political statements in this Eclogue, thinking poetry the wrong place for politics. It is therefore all the more interesting to discover the original version of the Eclogue was even more political and had to be quite radically changed, not least because the Tory editor of the Dorset County Chronicle objected[149]. Thus in the original version, John praises the charity of the parson and the squire and their good ladies in typical Barnesian fashion (as we have seen in Chapter Five):

> Var thee dost know the pa'son an' the squier
> Do git us coals to miake a bit o' vire,
> An' gi'e us many a meaty buone to pick,
> An' zend us medicine when we be zick,
> An' then ther liadies, bless their lives,
> Do come an' gi'e things to our wives...

But John goes on to warn Tom:

> You'll blunder out o' water into mud:
> A civil war wo'd be noo benefit
> To noobody, an' ef a man can't git
> Good bread by zweat,'e woon't, I think, by blood.

Tom goes on to defend his viewpoint, with which John disagrees:

> ...Ev'ry oone is var hizzelf, mind John.
> Zoo be the men that ya da'pend upon;
> But God ya know is var us al'.

---

[149] Bernard Jones, *The Poems* Vol.I, pp. xiii–xv

Given Barnes' total lack of support for party politics, it may seem pointless to wonder whom he would vote for at an election, were he alive today. Nevertheless it may help us to put him into perspective.

His rejection of Tory Imperialism would certainly have made him no friend of their opportunistic, ideological heirs on the left of the contemporary Conservative Party, the pro-Europeans. Barnes was too patriotic, too pro-English, nay, too pro-Dorset, to have become pro-European. Barnes had principles, he disliked capital, 'gold'. He disliked extremes of rich and poor: 'It is true that a man may now leave his wife a million of money earned for him by workmen in the service of his capital, but then fewer men out of every hundred in his trade may leave their children a hundred pounds'.[150] On the other hand his rejection of Big Business, of the division of labour and of Free Trade, and advocacy of Protectionism (the lack of which caused so much suffering in the rural society of nineteenth century England through the import of cheap corn from the vast prairie-lands of North America) would put him very far from free-marketeers on the right of the contemporary Conservative Party.

Would Barnes then, with his paternalism, his hope for social justice and the importance he placed, as a pedagogue, on Education, have found himself on the left of the political spectrum? After all, did he not preach 'Small is Beautiful' and the values of cottage industry?

We think not. Barnes could scarcely have been on the left. As we have seen, he was opposed to the Chartists. He felt that the Chartists would unsettle Dorset farmworkers without actually solving their problems. Thus he would have been against the organisation of Trade Unions, fearing their militancy; he believed strongly in self-help not State intervention – though it is true that he would have liked a national system to replace the Poor Laws. He did not believe that an idle man should receive money, but that he should work for them – he believed, not in welfare, but in workfare. He also disliked secular education, wanting a strong Church influence on the educational system. He felt that social injustice

---

[150] *VLG* p.70

could be resolved without militancy. Moreover, though Barnes saw the need for social justice, he saw it as coming from 'the law of Christian kindness', not from the works of humanistic and often atheistic thinkers, the most extreme of whom was Marx. Moreover, his Christian faith, though making him want social justice, also made him conservative, or rather traditional, in terms of personal morality and responsibility. He was opposed to divorce and we can imagine that he would have rejected outright even the possibility of abortion, let alone other morally permissive legislative changes. And, significantly, these have been introduced in our own times in a consensus by both Conservative and Labour governments, as if to demonstrate how little difference there is between them at least in this field.

Would then Barnes have found a place as a centrist? We think not, for Barnes was never wishy-washy. He was a man of deep principles, traditional in family matters, but looked for balance and justice in social and economic affairs – and as we have already mentioned, he saw this balance coming from an enlightened – Christian – squirearchy.

We have in fact then confirmed our initial intuition that speculation as to how Barnes would vote were he alive today, is indeed pointless. What then can be our conclusion of Barnes' political views?

Barnes was too deep and principled a thinker to feel comfortable in a political party. He was a man of tradition, not simply a conservative, though we might on the one hand be tempted to call him a Christian or High Tory in the sense that he believed in paternalism – source of social justice. But then, on the other hand, Barnes' paternalism was such that we might be tempted to call him a 'proto-socialist'. His politics were not so much linear as circular, for his Old Tory paternalism was that of social justice. Indeed in modern jargon, were he alive today, he might perhaps have been called a 'communitarian', but in a much deeper and sincerer sense than those who glibly label themselves with this term today – as we have seen in his original version of 'The Times': 'But God ya know is *var us al*'. What can be more communitarian than this? The Fatherhood of God brings the

Brotherhood of Man. Again in his poem 'Fellowship' he wrote of this sense of community so much stronger among the poor than among the rich:

> But we, wherever we do come,
> Ha' fellowship o' hands wi' lwoads,
> An' fellowship o' veet on roads,
> An' lowliness ov house an' hwome,
> An' fellowship in hwomely feäre,
> An' hwomely clothes vor daily wear;
> An' zoo mid [so might] Heaven bless the mwore
> The worken poor wi' fellowship.

As we have already seen, Barnes regretted the loss of the Old English elite, the 'atheldom' or nobility of Saxon England, who alone respected and were respected by the Saxon folk. And much of the tragedy in English society was the absence of an elite organically – racially – linked to the people and the presence of a foreign elite, an ultimately Norman-imposed Establishment. Not, after eight centuries, Norman by race, but Norman by value. One writer and poet working a full generation after Barnes' death, Maurice Hewlett, put it thus: 'The governing class is by race even now preponderatingly Latin-French with a Scandinavian admixture; by tradition, breeding and education it is entirely so. All the apparatus, all the science, all the circumstances of government are still Norman'.[151]

Barnes in fact envisioned a society so traditional that there would be no need for socialism; the folk of England would have found it in the 'law of Christian kindness' as applied by the protective lord of the Saxon hall and the fatherly married priest of the Saxon church, both lost with the imposition of feudalism, the Norman baron with his castle and the Norman warrior-bishop with his palace. For the spiritual rebirth of Saxon lords and Saxon priests Barnes looked to an enlightened nineteenth century Christian squirearchy and clergy. In fact Barnes' politics were Saxon politics. This is why he can in no way be fitted into the party political system, either of his time or of

---

[151] Maurice Hewlett, Preface to '*The Song of the Plow*', 1916

ours. This is why he can be called both a populist and a traditionalist. Barnes was outside the system, and probably felt politics to be needless. Social and economic justice would not be delivered by political hacks (and it is true that they never have been) but only by an elite of 'squires' and clergy incarnating 'the law of Christian kindness'. His Saxon social and economic values amounted to Saxon politics, which can perhaps be best summed up by his own thoroughly unpolitical confession of faith: 'My work is peace and salvation'.[152]

Politically Barnes confessed a strand of English patriotism that runs discreetly and often unseen throughout English history, culture and thought. As a postscriptum to this overview of Barnes' political vision and values, it is not without interest to ask whether he has any followers today. Curiously enough, and only recently, one Member of Parliament has spoken in a way which reflects some considerable part of Barnes' views. A contemporary rebel, Sir Richard Body, has written thus: 'Surely Englishness is grounded on Anglo-Saxon values. Before the Normans came to conquer and corrupt, England was far more democratic than today; everyone's voice was heard in a society of plain living and plain speaking, where extremes of personal wealth and poverty were not permitted, and where personal freedom abounded, blended with a sense of community. The Anglo-Saxons were libertarian, and believed in vigorous freedom of speech, which led to truth in a trial by jury, as much as in the Witan (the Anglo-Saxon Parliament)... Snobbish, conformist, pageant-adoring and hard of heart, the Normans introduced a contrast... the Norman tradition – conformist, regulated and authoritarian'.[153] Now if the reader has followed our thought so far, but is not yet convinced, let him look at the words 'plain speaking' and then turn to Part Two of this work: *The Rebirth of English.*

---

[152] Sermon on the Day of Humiliation
[153] *New Statesman & Society*

Part Two

The Rebirth of English

Chapter 8

The English Language

I am... a 'lingual conservative'; and it is therefore that I wish to see the English a purer, and more self-enriched tongue, instead of being a jargon made up of four or five others.

William Barnes, 'Formation of the English Language', Supp. Vol. CIII of the *Gentleman's Magazine*, pp. 591–2, 1833

Short words are best and the old words when short are best of all.

Sir Winston Churchill, 2 November, 1949

Following the Norman Invasion of 1066, the English language was invaded by French words which replaced English words. This new vocabulary concerned above all the matters which concerned the Norman ruling class. Thus the vocabulary of Government, Law, Religion and Military matters are still largely Norman-French. English words were displaced and replaced. Thus, for example, by the fourteenth century Chaucer used nearly 500 French words in the Prologue to his Canterbury Tales.[154] The fact that English has two different sets of words for animals and the meat of animals is very telling: the fact that we say cow, calf, pig, deer and sheep indicates simply that the peasants who bred such animals were English, whereas the words beef, veal, pork, venison and mutton indicate that those who ate the meat of those animals were the Norman masters. The Norman outlook and Norman traditions even today belong to the British Establishment, be it through the names and blood of the 'English' (or rather Norman) aristocracy, the Norman-founded public schools, Norman-founded Oxbridge and the predominance of graduates from both in Westminster, Whitehall, the Established Anglican Church and the officer-elite in the armed forces. This is not to mention the extensive use of Norman-Latin by barristers, the prestige associated

---

[154] See *The Cambridge Encyclopaedia of The English Language* by David Crystal (1995), p.47

with the knowledge of Latin and French and subsequent use of Latin and French expressions by the elite. Even the toffee-nosed accent associated until recently with 'R.P.' or 'B.B.C. English', the accent of the upper class, is merely a Norman accent, that of invaders who could not speak English properly and then, ironically, passed on their accent to succeeding generations as a status symbol, the sign of their superiority and prestige over the English peasantry. Wrote the poet Maurice Hewlett: 'The Norman Conquest, that successful raid made a conquest... was when foreigners acquired an ascendancy, which they have never yet dropped'.[155]

Now historically there have been many who objected to the Norman Invasion. Immediately after the Invasion, their resistance took the form of armed struggle. Later, however, their resistance to the Normans took other, more subtle forms. For example in the seventeenth century a Protestant merchant-class, overthrowing an outdated monarchy in a civil war, justified itself by claiming that it was casting off the Norman Yoke imposed by the Conqueror. Unfortunately, though they threw off a high-tax tyranny (and William the Conqueror's rule had certainly been tyrannical and high-taxing), their revolt had not been radical enough to go any further. However, the form of resistance that we shall deal with here is not political but linguistic.

In the sixteenth century the Elizabethan thinker and writer Sir John Cheke (1514–57) wrote: 'Our own tung should be written cleare and pure, unmixt and unmangeled with borrowing of other tunges'. He was closely followed by a disciple, Roger Ascham (1515–68), who promoted 'the Englyshe tongue' as opposed to Latin and Greek and expressed himself in the lively, pure speech of the common people. The famous writer Edmund Spenser (1552?–1599) also sympathised with Saxon English. And in the seventeenth century the Levellers not only sought a denormanising of the political system by a return to the Old English communitarianism, but they also sought to cleanse English of Norman words. William Camden (1551–1623) leant his weight, writing: 'The olde English could express most aptly all the conceiptes

---

[155] Maurice Hewlett in the Preface to 'The Song of the Plow', 1916

of the minde in their own tongue without borrowing from any other'.[156]
And in the seventeenth century, writers like Sir John Hare and Francis
Whyte spoke of the matchlessness of 'the Saxon tongue' and called for
French words to be purged from the tongue and 'be replaced with
words from the old Saxon'. It is to this stream of thought and resistance
that William Barnes belonged. Since his time, and indeed partly
through his influence, others have joined this current of thought. They
include the Archbishop of Dublin, Richard Trench who in 1855 wrote
'English Past and Present' and writers such as Dickens, Morris, Hardy,
Hopkins, Orwell and the linguist and historian of English, Jespersen.
They all suggested that English could have remained free of Latinisms
and that English justifies itself only as long as it grows organically from
its own Anglo-Saxon or Old English roots. Hopkins, for example,
wrote: 'It makes one weep to think what English might have been'.[157]
No-one, however, has ever taken these ideas as far as William Barnes.
Thus although William Morris invented the word 'songcraft' to replace
the word 'poetry' – Barnes invented hundreds of words from English
roots and stems to replace foreign words, he remade 'Saxon English',
swimming against the linguistic tide of English history, doing the
opposite to what the Normans did after their Invasion. Just as he
wished England and the English to return to their true English roots, so
he wished to see the English tongue return to its true English roots.
What exactly were his motives?

Firstly, having been brought up in the first years of the nineteenth
century in the Blackmore Vale, an isolated area of England, isolated
even for Dorset, Barnes as a child had spoken a form of English
which contained few words of foreign origin. He had been brought up
in the still largely 'Saxon' pre-industrial world and the speech of that
world, the Dorset dialect, 'the Tory of languages', was still basically
a late form of Old English, which the nineteenth century generally
called 'Saxon' or 'Anglo-Saxon'. From childhood observation he had
heard that people spoke one way but at school he had learnt to write
in another. Thus people said:

---

[156] *Remaines*, p.25
[157] Dugdale, p.206

I can't bear it.
I can see it in my mind's eye.
You can take that two ways.
You can't get away from it.
He may well come.

But they were taught to write:

This is intolerable.
I imagined it.
That is ambiguous.
This is inevitable.
He will probably arrive.

The speech is simple, with short, English words: the written language contains long, Latin words. In Dorset this was even more the case than with Standard English, for the Dorset dialect had kept many words lost to Standard English through their displacement by Latin words. The Dorset dialect of the yeoman-farmer in Barnes' time was almost pure English. As he later wrote: 'We cannot wonder at the purity of the western dialects, as we must see that the minds of the rustic families of west Saxony, the proper title of the contracted 'Wessex', were as little exposed to the leaven of the old French of the Norman court, as they have been in later times to that of the Latin of the learned, or the so-thought elegant French of the polite; and so while the land-holding Norman families, whether Harcourts, Percies, Nevilles, St. Los, or others, retained their Latin-French tongue, the wood-girt and hill-sheltered tuns (or country-houses) of the West were still vocal with the purest Saxon in which the Norman Conquest itself was recorded in the Saxon Chronicle'.[158]

Certainly the next stage in Barnes' development must have been his phenomenal linguistic studies which started in his teens. His study of Latin and then other Romance languages, especially French, would have led him to realise how English had been shaped after the Norman Invasion. But in studying the Germanic languages, including

---

[158] Scrapbook 2, p.34 in the Dorset County Museum

the Frisian that is so close to what English might have been had the Normans been pushed back into the sea, he would at once have realised that English is a Germanic, Teutonic tongue. His study of history would have confirmed this. Once he had begun studying Old English, Anglo-Saxon, then he would have seen all. Moreover, his discovery of Welsh quite early on and subsequent visits to Wales had given him the vision of a 'pure' language, expressive and uncontaminated by borrowings from foreign languages. As early as 1828 in letters to the Dorset County Chronicle signed 'Linguiana' he was calling for a 'pure' English, freed from non-English words. Of his thoughts on this, we have a clear record. 'I have before me one hundred and fifty so taken English law-words which were brought into the English courts with the Norman French tongue; but English speech did not therefore become richer by so many words, because most of them thrust aside English ones... King Alfred gave to English minds the matter of Gregory's Pastoral (King Alfred's translation of St. Gregory the Great's book, 'Pastoral Care') with a greater share (nearly all) of pure English words, than most English scholars could now find for it'.[159] And in conversation with his daughter on the word 'geäte' (Dorset for 'gate'), he remarked: 'Observe that word. That is how King Alfred would have pronounced it, and how it was called in the 'Saxon Chronicle', which tells us of King Edward (St. Edward the Martyr), who was slain at Corfe's 'geäte'. Ah! If the court had not moved to London, then the speech of King Alfred of which our Dorset is the remnant – would have been – the court language of today, and it would have been more like Anglo-Saxon than it is today'.[160]

Interestingly, these thoughts influenced Thomas Hardy, who got his idea of 'Wessex' directly from Barnes, to say: "It has often seemed to me a pity, from many points of view – and from the point of view of language – among the rest – that Winchester did not remain, as it once was, the royal, political and social capital of England, leaving London to be the commercial capital... In that case, neither of them

---

[159] *Speech-craft*, p.87
[160] Baxter, pp.316-7

would have been so monstrously overgrown as London is today... We should then have had a metropolis free from the fogs of the Thames Valley... and we might have preserved a larger proportion of the racy Saxon of the West Country"[161].

In fact Barnes realised that the Dorset dialect of his childhood was actually descended from the language of the Court of King Alfred the Great. And he found it superior in the softness and mellowness of its elisions and contractions to 'London' English. There is more euphony ('sound-sweetness') in the Dorset dialect 'housen' than 'houses' and, from his own invented English, 'forbend' is certainly softer than 'deflect'. Barnes wrote: 'The author, however, is not ashamed to say, that after reading some of the best compositions of many of the most polished languages, he can contemplate its pure and strong Saxon features with perfect satisfaction, and has often found the simple truths enunciated in the pithy sentences of village patriarchs only expanded, by the weaker wordiness of modern compositions, into high-sounding paragraphs'.[162]

The third stage in Barnes' development must be as a pedagogue, and Barnes was an excellent one, loved by his pupils, of whom many went far in career thanks to him. Now, Barnes was a teacher at the time of the Industrial Revolution, a time of swift social change, including educational change. Although compulsory education came in only at the end of his life, he had spent nearly forty years in the teaching profession. He had always wanted his pupils to understand what he was saying – and thus he faced the dilemma of all pedagogues – how could he put across complex ideas in a simple way and in a simple language? Perhaps it was this that prompted him to write: 'The English are a great nation; and as an Englishman, I am sorry that we have not a language of our own; but that whenever we happen to conceive a thought above that of a plough-boy, or produce anything beyond a pitch-fork, we are obliged to borrow a word from others before we can utter it, or give it a name; and to conclude, as

---

[161] R. T. Hopkins, *Thomas Hardy's Dorset*, London 1922, pp.156-7
[162] *Poems of Rural Life in the Dorset Dialect*, pp.48-9

the English language is most rich in literature of every kind, our writers should aim to purify and fix it, for if they go on corrupting it, their own writings after some time, will not be read without a glossary, perhaps not at all'.[163]

On the subject of the importance of Anglo-Saxon he wrote in an article of 1847: 'To neglect wholly the language and writings of our forefathers seems like the folly of a crew who would tear out an authentic leaf of their logbook because it was not written by the hands that filled up the rest'.[164] Barnes wanted the innovations of the nineteenth century to have not Latin or Greek names, but English ones. Names of Latin or Greek origin in English he called not English but 'Englandish'. And the common people could not understand this foreign English – the source of so many of Dickens' 'Malapropisms'. He wanted to breathe new life, power, beauty and value into English through the English roots of English. This is why he called himself a 'revolutionary'; he wanted ' a rebellion against standard Latinised English', he 'asked for a Renaissance of the native English language'[165]. As was Barnes' wont, by being traditional, he was being *radical* – going to the roots of English. Thus, when Thomas Hardy showed Barnes' one of the first 'bicycles', Barnes' reaction was immediately to object to the word 'bicycle' and coin the word 'wheelsaddle'. And frankly do we not now regret failing to use the word 'wheelsaddle' instead of 'bicycle'? We can at once visualise a 'wheelsaddle', but 'bicycle' is a purely abstract concept. In the same way for 'omnibus' Barnes invented 'folkwain'. What could be simpler or more concrete?

Barnes opposed the linguistic establishment and probably his greatest mental adversary was Dr. Johnson who in his ultra-Latinate dictionary represented all that was bad in English, the obsession with words of non-English origin which remained an incomprehensible

---

[163] *Gentleman's Magazine*, Supp. Vol. CII, 1832, 'On Compounds in the English Language'

[164] 'Guide to the Anglo-Saxon Tongue' (Review), *Gentleman's Magazine*, February 1847, p.178

[165] Jacobs, pp.12 and 61

jargon to the unschooled. In this Barnes saw the class snobbery of the period – one who littered his speech with Gallicisms and Latinisms thought he was showing off his newly attained knowledge, in the same way that today someone from the Third World or Eastern Europe shows off by littering his speech with Americanisms. In fact, however, such people were not showing off their knowledge, but their ignorance. As Barnes, familiar with some seventy languages and author of ninety-five books and articles, mainly on language, wrote: 'The truth is, that, till lately, the learned commonly studied few other languages, but the Latin and Greek; and thus knowing little of the Gothic (Germanic) languages, and therefore not understanding the nature and powers of the Saxon part of the English, they neglected it as a useless relic of a rude tongue, of which nothing could be made; and, as extending science brought in a need of new words, they took them from those two great tongues of antiquity, when they might have made them from simples of their own'.[166] And again, written in his own Saxon English as if to prove his point: 'English has become a more mongrel speech [hybrid language] by the needless inbringing [unnecessary introduction] of words from Latin, Greek and French, instead of words which might have been found in its older form, or in the speech of landfolk [country-people] over all England, or might have been formed from its own roots and stems, as wanting [missing] words have been formed in German and other purer tongues. Thence English has become so much harder to learn, that, in its foreign-worded fullness, it is a speech only for the more learned, and foreign to unschooled men, so that the sermon and book are half-lost to their minds... Some of the mongrel form of our English has arisen from the slighting [denigration] of Saxon-English, and other Teutonic tongues at our universities and in our schools...'.[167]

Barnes knew enough about Germanic and Slavic languages, let alone the Non-Indo-European ones, to realise that English could also be used to make learned compounds. Indeed a mere knowledge of Old

---

[166] *Gentleman's Magazine*, Supp. Vol. CII, 1832, 'On Compounds in the English Language'

[167] *Early England and the Saxon English*, p.101

English was enough to confirm this: thus in Old English, 'modest' is 'shamefast', 'pious' is 'awefast', 'honourable' is 'aweworthy', 'hospitable' is guestly', 'flattery' is 'lightwords', 'mediceine' is 'leechdom', 'temporary' is 'whilewendly', 'orthodox' is 'beliefful', 'secular' is 'worldkind', religious' is 'godkind', 'possessed' is 'devilsick' and 'merciful' is 'mildhearted'. Old English was a literary language, particularly developed in its West Saxon or Wessex form. It had plenty of learned compounds to express religious, philosophical or other concepts. The tragedy was that the learned compounds had been lost at the Norman Invasion when the learned class was lost – through genocide, exile and dispossession, 'whereas in Tuscany and in the west of Ireland, or in Wales, the speech of the upper ranks is that of the cottage, and the well-worded book of the higher mind needs no list of hard words to open its meaning to the lower'.[168] As a teacher Barnes wanted his pupils to understand English. For this reason he wanted to see a new phonetic alphabet (he himself wrote in 'phonography') and, above all, he published several works. Barnes' aim was pedagogical in books such as *The Etymological Glossary or easy Expositor for the use of Schools and Non-Latinists* (published in 1829, when Barnes was only 28), *Elements of English Grammar* (1849), *Se Gefylsta* (the first ever Grammar of Anglo-Saxon for use in schools) (1849), *TIW; or, A View of the Roots and Stems of English as a Teutonic Tongue* (1862), not to mention his major linguistic works on languages in general or his later works on grammar and philosophy actually written in his own 'Saxon English', or a host of short articles and letters on the same subject published in journals and newspapers.

Apart from his didactic work as a schoolteacher for thirty-nine years, we should not overlook his didactic work for almost exactly the same period as a priest – and a priest with a most compassionate heart, who literally suffered with his flock. Just as he wanted schoolchildren to understand, so, as a priest, he wanted his flock to understand his preaching. 'The Latin and Greek mingled-speech of the pulpit is often one ground on which the poor leave their church, where the

---

[168] op. cit.

preaching is, as they call it, too high for them… Many a clergyman, who would not think of giving orders to his man-servant in terms which that person could not understand, is yet accustomed every Sunday to address a rustic congregation in discourses which would be just as intelligible to it if they were preached in Hebrew. What we want for the pulpit, as well as for the book, and the platform, for the people, is a pure, homely, strong Saxon-English of English stems, such as would be understood by common English minds and touch English hearts'.[169] Elsewhere he repeated much the same: 'The Latinish and Greekish wording [Greek terminology] is a hindrance to the teaching of the homely poor, or at least the landfolk [country-people]. It is not clear to them, and some of them say of a clergyman that his Latinised preaching is too high for them, and seldom seek the church'.[170] Since Barnes was no hypocrite, and literally practised what he preached: 'he preached many a sermon, not in Dorset, as one of his critics has said, but in that terse Saxon-English which to strangers sounded so quaint, but was quite plain to the simplest villagers'.[171] And the Bishop of Salisbury, visiting him with the Holy Communion at the end of Barnes' life wrote of Barnes' 'own terse and graceful, though homely words'.[172]

We have then considered the origins of Barnes' attraction to 'Saxon English', both through growing up in Dorset, but also as a linguist of genius, teacher and priest. He considered that English should be composed of English words because as such it was more easily understandable and more expressive. Each language should keep faith with its own spirit and genius. However, there is yet another aspect of his interest, and that is as a poet. For many this will be the most important aspect of all, for it is as a poet that Barnes' fame now chiefly lies.

As a poet Barnes was sensitive to speech. Barnes' poetry is closely linked with his love of language, especially his love of the Dorset

---

[169] op. cit., p.106
[170] *Speech-craft*, p.88
[171] Baxter, p.206
[172] op. cit., p.322

dialect. When his daughter wrote his biography she wrote of 'William Barnes Poet and Philologist' and she noted in that book that her father first began writing his dialect poems in the 'hope of preserving, and dream of restoring this pure ancient language'.[173] In his *Early England and the Saxon-English* of 1869, Barnes put into words a truth that he had practised all his life: 'We want... a pure, homely, strong Saxon-English of English stems, such as would be understood by common English minds and touch English hearts... We should not reach the English mind or heart the more readily by turning 'He scattered his foes' into 'He dissipated his inimical forces'.[174] Here Barnes touches on a fundamental fact that none can deny, that the language of English poetry, that which speaks to the heart is Anglo-Saxon English, the English whose roots are Old English. A poet uses the words that speak to the heart, and those words are those of our distant forebears before the coming of the Normans.

And Barnes was most sensitive to the past. He kept faith with his forebears. Some of his happiest moments were spent at the deserted village of Farringdon near Winterborne Came, where he would lose himself in contemplation before the still visible ruins of the ancient village church. About it he wrote a poem 'The Depopulated Village'. It symbolises his communion with the past and to what extent Barnes was absent from the present, but taking part in the past – and also the future. Barnes' fascination with language is why his daughter described his book *Speech-Craft*, written in the most pure Saxon English, as 'one of his favourite mind-children'.[175] The poet Coventry Patmore wrote of Barnes: 'He acquired so extensive an acquaintance with languages... in order to satisfy a profound delight in contemplating those obscure echoes and imitations of realities, by which language in its infancy is rendered almost pure poetry, and to feel and preserve the magic charm which is the poet's greatest art when he has to deal with the fully-developed tongue'.[176] As a recent

---

[173] Chedzoy, Fore Word to *Poems Grave and Gay*, p.v
[174] *Early England and the Saxon English*, pp.106-7
[175] Baxter, p.275
[176] *St. James' Gazette*, 9th October 1886

commentator has quoted, this is very much the charm of Barnes' poetry: 'When you open his book down from the shelf, you can smell the mint in the fields, just as it was in his day'.[177]

'Speechlore [philology] can already show the work of the great Mind of Minds... A first and pure speech was not made up of words cackled into shape by the strained utterances of passionate monkey-men, but it was formed from a few root-sounds in the most admirable and regular order'.[178] In speaking thus, William Barnes not only explained his interest in human language but also denounced the then fashionable theories of Darwin. Words differentiated men from animals, for language is the sign of the immortal soul breathed into man by the *Word* of God. The purity and regularity of speech was a sign of its closeness to the Creator. Its 'mongrelisation' was the result of the sins of men. Hence Barnes' search for linguistic purity. He was without doubt one of the most brilliant linguistic geniuses in English history and much of his solitary but inspired work regarding Indo-European languages, English etymology and place-names was pioneering, retaining its validity even today. And yet he was cruelly snubbed by the linguistic establishment, including the compiler of the Oxford English Dictionary, Furnivall, who was then at work.[179] Barnes was too radical for the Establishment – his rejection of heavy Latinate Victorian English came too early. Thus in his last work, 'A Glossary of the Dorset Dialect, he poked gentle fun at the Establishment by 'translating' the diplomatic jargon of the Queen's Speech of 1884 into the honest simplicity of Dorset. An extract reads: 'I continue to view with unabated satisfaction the mitigation and diminution of agrarian crime in Ireland, and the substantial improvement in the condition of its people'. Barnes' version reads: 'I do still zee to my unlessened happiness how vield crimes be a milden'd and a lessen'd in Ireland, and in what a soundly bettered plight be the vo'k'.[180]

---

[177] S. F. C. Williams, 'Barnes as a Free-thinker', *Dorset* No.85
[178] *The Hawk*, October 1867, p.298
[179] See Jacobs, especially pp.72-78
[180] *A Glossary of the Dorset Dialect*, p.viii

Barnes was a Nature-lover and therefore could not tolerate artifice, including in speech. As we have seen at the end of Part Two, because he loved Nature he was a patriot. He could also be called a 'language-patriot', for his home-love made him also love the speech of the Saxon English, reflected in the dialect of Dorset folk. Saxon English was poetic English, it was the English of his 'hwomely rhymes' and his sermons, which his congregations understood and whose hearts were touched. The Saxon English of Dorset was the speech of Alfred the Great, of St. Edward the Martyr, of Wessex and therefore the speech of Old English literature, culture and civilisation. And something similar could also be said of South Saxon (Sussex dialect), Middle Saxon (Middlesex dialect), East Saxon (Essex dialect) and even the Anglian dialects of Mercia (the Midlands), East Anglia and Northumbria. (Certainly several of the dialect words that the present author has read in Barnes' poetry are the same as those in his own East Saxon dialect).

In Barnes' Saxonising of Latinate English, his wish for purity of speech, there was no crude nationalism (as there was in Hitler's language policies in the Germany of the 1930s). Barnes was never crude, but a fine patriot. What he stood against was not the use of foreign words for foreign things but the use of foreign words for English things. Thus after the Norman Invasion, ''judge' took the stead of 'dema'; 'cause' of 'sac'; 'bail' of 'borh'; and the lawyers said 'arson', for 'forburning'; 'burglary', for 'housebreach'; and 'carrucate', for 'ploughland''.[181] The use of Norman-French and Latin was only the expression of Norman arrogance and Norman ignorance. It was the pride and contempt of the invader for the invaded, an ignorance of the native, English culture, it was cultural and linguistic imperialism.

To prove his point Barnes wrote several works in his Saxonising English, in particular we might mention, *Early England and the Saxon-English*. However, there were two works written almost completely in Saxon English, these were his work on English

---

[181] *Speech-craft*, p.87

Grammar – *Speech-Craft* – and Logic – *Rede-Craft*. He described the former as, 'a small trial... towards the upholding of our own strong old Anglo-Saxon speech... I hope that the little book may afford a few glimpses of new insight into our fine old Anglo-Saxon tongue... I have tried to teach English by English, and so have given English words for most of the lore-words [scientific terms], as I believe they would be more readily and more clearly understood... there are tokens that, ere long the English youth will want an outline of the Greek and Latin tongues ere he can well understand his own speech'.[182] Barnes showed great courage in doing this – he could after all have written about topics such as farming or thatching. But this would have been a fraud, for Barnes well knew that most of the vocabulary of these topics is 'Saxon English' anyway. He wanted to write about subjects that are full of Latinisms, to truly prove his point that English could be much more English and therefore less Latin than it conventionally was.

Having then set out why Barnes wanted to purify English of the non-native, it is now our task to analyse how exactly he went about this 'Rebirth of English'

---

[182] Quoted in Jacobs, p.42

Chapter 9

Methodology

Though self-taught, William Barnes was one of the greatest linguistic scholars of his day, receiving the visits of the French linguist Prince Lucien Bonaparte and the admiration of the Oxford pioneer Max Müller. Familiar with some seventy languages from several language groups, he spoke and wrote fourteen fluently. In his *An Investigation of the Laws of Case in Language* (1840), he had begun to look for clues to a universal grammar and in *A Philological Grammar* (1854) he even attempted to write a key to all languages. He kept a personal diary, at first in Welsh, Spanish or German and later, for many years, in Italian. Thus Barnes' approach to the question of recovering a 'Saxon English' could only be scientific, the professional, etymological approach of the philologist. In what did it consist and how did he recreate Saxon English?

Translation and Analogy

One of Barnes methods was to create new words by analogy with other languages. This involved breaking down vocabulary into its component parts (roots, prefixes and suffixes) and translating it by analogy with other languages. In analysing Barnes' techniques in the field of word-creation we shall first of all look at two lists made up of prefixes and of suffixes, including actual examples of word-building.

1 Barnes' Translations of Foreign Prefixes

Foreign Prefix	English Prefix	Examples with Meanings	
		Foreign	*English*
ad-	on-	adhere	oncleave
ambi-	twy-	ambiguous	twymeaning
an-	for	analyse	forloosen
	mis-	anachronism	mistiming
anti-	fore-	anticipate	forestall
arch-	head-	archbishop	headbishop
bi-	two-	bilateral	two-sided
co-	up-	coherent	upcleaving
col-		collision	upclashing
con-		conclusion	upshot
contra-	gain-	contradict	gainsay
de-	for-	define	formark
	off-	determine	offmark
	out-	describe	outmark
	un-	develop	unfold
demo-	folk-	democracy	folkdom
dis-	sunder-	dispose	sunderset
	for-	disrupt	forbreak
	off-	distinguish	offmark
	out-	disperse	outsend
equi-	even-	equality	evenhood
ex-	out-	exclude	outshut
mono-	lone-	monotony	lonesound

Foreign Prefix	English Prefix	Examples with Meanings Foreign	English
multi-	many-	multiple	manifold
per-	for-	perfect	fordone
poly-	many-	polygamist	manywedder
pre-	fore-	predict	foretell
pseudo-	sham-	pseudo-sailor	sham-sailor
re-	again-	repeat	say again
	back-	reflect	backshine
	with-	revolve	withwind
semi-	half-	semi-circle	half-circle
trans-	over-	transitive	overfaresome
	through-	transparent	through-showing
ver- (German)	for-	annihilate	fornaughten (German = vernichten)

2 Barnes' Translations of Foreign Suffixes

Foreign Suffix	English Suffix	Examples with Meanings Foreign	English
-bar (German)	-some	edible	eatsome (German = essbar)
-cracy	-dom	democracy	folkdom
-cy	-hood	regency	regenthood
-ible	-some	flexible	bendsome

2 Barnes' Translations of Foreign Suffixes (continued)

Foreign Suffix	English Suffix	Examples with Meanings	
		Foreign	English
-ics	-lore	tactics	warlore
-ify	-en	clarify	clearen
-ism	-hood	absenteeism	absenteehood
	-ishness	Latinism	Latinishness
-ity	-hood	equality	evenhood
-lich (German)	-ly	royal	kingly (German = königlich)
-ography	-writ	biography	lifewrit
-ology,	-lore	ornithology	birdlore
-onomy		astronomy	starlore
-sam (German)	-some	tedious	longsome (German = langsam (slow))
-scope	-seer	microscope	closeseer
-ty	-hood	royalty	kinghood

3 Barnes' Translations of Latin Roots

Once he had established translations of foreign prefixes and suffixes, it was then necessary to translate foreign roots used in English, or, as Barnes would have said, in Englandish:

Latin	*English*	*Examples with Meanings*	
Root	*Root*	*Latin*	*English*
flect	bend	flexible	bendsome
ject	cast	eject	outcast
pose	put	preposition	foreputting
tract	draw	distract	offdraw
voke	call	evoke	call out
volve	wind	revolve	withwind

Through the extension of this technique applied to translation and analogy with French and German roots, other new words could be found for old and 'Englandish' be replaced by English:

French Roots	*English*	*Englandish*
Lieu + tenant	Steadholder	Lieutenant

German Word	*English*	*Englandish*
arbeitsam	worksome	industrious
Jahrhundert	yearhundred	century
möglich	mayly	possible
Wortbuch	wordbook	dictionary
Zahnarzt	toothdoctor	dentist
Zeitwort	timeword	verb

With regard to analogies with German roots, Barnes was particularly fond of the analogy between the English suffix -'some' and the German 'sam' (found in several Germanic languages), meaning 'inclined to', 'disposed to', 'tending to be'. Thus on the basis of the Standard English awesome, blithesome, burdensome, cumbersome, fearsome, frolicsome, fulsome, handsome, irksome, loathsome, meddlesome, quarrelsome, tiresome, troublesome, wearisome and wholesome, Barnes took from dialect and above all invented:

actsome	active	loosensome	laxative
aimsome	single-minded	lovesome	affectionate
allsome	universal	marksome	definite
ayesome	positive	matchsome	definite
barksome	'yappy'	maysome	possible
becomesome	developmental	mightsome	probable
bendsome	flexible	moansome	mournful
bethanksome	thankful	naysome	negative
breaksome	fragile	needsome	necessary
breathesome	breathable	onesome	singular
cheatsome	false	outshutsome	exclusive
darksome	darkening	overfaresome	transitive
doingsome	active	overthwartsome	opposite
eatsome	edible	playsome	playful
fallsome	deciduous	runsome	liquid
fightsome	aggressive	sharesome	particular
frightsome	frightening	sparesome	frugal
growsome	fertile	speaksome	garrulous
guilesome	illusory	sundersome	separable
halesome	salubrious	talksome	talkative
happensome	accidental	teachsome	didactic
hearsome	obedient	toilsome	diligent
heedsome	attentive	twaysome	equivocal
hindersome	obstructive	usesome	useful
huntsome	fond of hunting	withstandsome	resistant
laughsome	inclined to laughter	wontsome	common
		worksome	industrious
longsome	tedious	yieldsome	compliant

4 Revival of Obsolete Words

Another method of word-creation was to revive the obsolete or obsolescent:

Englandish	English	Englandish	English
arbitrator	daysman	musician	gleeman
desecrate	unhallow	plant	wort
girl	maiden	pleasant	winsome
merchant	chapman		

5 Revival of Anglo-Saxon Roots

Another method was to create new words from Anglo-Saxon roots:

Englandish	English	Englandish	English
accustom	onwone	reason	rede
cemetery	licherest	school	lorehouse
equerry	horsethane	servant	thane
mathematics	rimecraft	slave	thrall
medicine	leechcraft	spiritual	ghostly
merciful	mildhearted	trinity	threeness
modest	shamefast	veracious	soothfast

6 Use of Dialect Words

Dialect words, of Saxon origin, could also replace 'Englandish'. Naturally, Barnes resorted especially to the Dorset dialect:

Englandish	English	Englandish	English
active	doughty	industrious	toilsome
autumn	fall	obliged	beholden
caution	forewit	solitary	lonesome
energetic	sprack	vibrate	whiver

7 The Use of Existing Words

Apart from these methods, Barnes also employed a far simpler one – that of taking words already in use but of 'Saxon' i.e. Old English origin to replace words used in English of Non-English, Latin or French, origin. Below we give some examples:

Words of Non-English Origin	Words of Old English Origin	Words of Non-English Origin	Words of Old English Origin
allow	let	deteriorate	worsen
action	deed	liberty	freedom
altitude	height	manual	handbook
annual	yearly	oblique	slanting
audible	hearable	ornithologist	birdwatcher
celestial	heavenly	reprimand	upbraid
continent	mainland	terminate	end
cruel	ruthless		

8 Extension of Meaning

Barnes also tried to extend the wordstock of English through extending the meaning of words already in use through adding new meanings or changing style or register. Thus for example he would use 'befoul' for 'contaminate', 'befriend' for 'acquaint', 'bemuddle' for 'confuse', 'heap up' for 'accumulate', 'weatherlore' for 'meteorology', 'middling' for 'mediocre', 'wilderness' for 'desert', 'wrangle' for 'argue'.

9 Formation of New Compounds

Finally, another method of forming neologisms was through forming new compounds. Barnes was keen on this and asked, since other Germanic languages had many compounds, why English did not have more of them. He deemed that there was no need to borrow because new words could be made from compounding roots and stems already in existence. One method Barnes used for creating new adjectives to describe human characteristics was to extend or simply use more often an already existing practice, as for example with kind-hearted', 'whole-hearted', 'like-minded', 'mean-spirited'. Thus:

comic	=	light-hearted
cordial	=	warm-hearted
courageous	=	stout-hearted
cowardly	=	faint-hearted
cruel	=	hard-hearted
melancholy	=	heavy-hearted
perverse	=	wrong-headed
liberal	=	free-minded
magnanimous	=	great-minded
pusillanimous	=	weak-minded
noble	=	lofty-thoughted or well-born
intelligent	=	quick-witted or sharp-witted
stupid	=	dull-witted or slow-witted

Conclusions

The only linguist to have shown any real interest in Barnes linguistic work, Willis D. Jacobs, wrote a modest volume on *William Barnes, Linguist* and a later article 'A Word-hoard for Folkdom' ('A Vocabulary for Democracy'). According to a sample he took, he reckoned that 43% of Barnes' new words were pure neologisms, based on Anglo-Saxon, 30% were restored obsolescent or neglected forms, 14% were of dialect origin, 7% restored Old English or Middle English terms and 6% were extensions to the meanings of standard words (*William Barnes, Linguist* p.72). What then can be said of Barnes' word-making? Were all his strivings simply the 'enthusiasm of a crank' or was this the genius of a great linguist? What were his successes and his failures?

Chapter 10

Success or Failure?

We shall first take a look at the criticisms which have been levelled at William Barnes' 'word-shapening', then go on to see what is worthy of praise, and finally draw conclusions.

Criticisms

1 Dead Roots Cannot Be Revived

All commentators are of the opinion that one once a language is dead, it cannot be revived. Given that this is so, it has to be conceded that once a root is dead or no longer active in a language, then it cannot be revived either. It seems to us that this is the case with a number of Barnes' neologisms, for example:

inwit = conscience

manqualm = epidemic

push-wainling = perambulator

Wain and qualm are both dead Old English roots which Modern English has lost. Although it may be argued that 'wit' is still active, 'inwit' is, perhaps unfortunately, not a word which is going to live. Barnes' critics mostly consider that the revival of dead roots made Barnes' enterprise seem quaint or even cranky and therefore many failed to take him seriously. Language is a living, organic creation; it cannot be artificially revived. This is perhaps the most serious accusation against Barnes and, indeed, against anyone who wishes to fight for linguistic purity.

2 Germanising

The second criticism of Barnes is that in trying to delatinise English, he germanised it. This is true as regards phrasal verbs, where often (though by no means consistently) Barnes in German style put phrasal verbs particles in front of the verb, instead of afterwards, as is normal in English. Thus:

Englandish	Barnes	English
accept	intake	take in
accumulate	upgather	gather up
contract	updraw	draw up
disseminate	outscatter	scatter out
elicit	outdraw	draw out
exhale	outbreathe	breathe out
omit	outleave	leave out
reject	offcast	cast off
supervise	overwatch	watch over

3 Unnecessary Neologisms

For some, Barnes got carried away with his 'word-making' and invented words from Saxon roots to replace Latin vocabulary needlessly: there already existed words of Anglo-Saxon origin which were quite adequate replacements. Thus:

Englandish	Barnes	English
accelerate	onquicken	speed up
ambiguous	twymeaning	two-sided
ancestors	fore-elders	forebears
attentive	heedsome	heedful
attract	fordraw	draw to
beauty	fairhood	loveliness
carnivorous	flesh-eatsome	meat-eating

Englandish	Barnes	English
dissuade	offsweeten	talk out of
edible	eatsome	eatable
false	guilesome	guileful
fragile	breaksome	breakable
garrulous	talksome	talkative
grateful	bethanksome	thankful
herbivorous	grass-eatsome	grass-eating
industrious	worksome	hard-working
instinct	ongoading	hunch
liquid	runsome	runny
necessary	needsome	needful
proceed	forthgo	head, make for
revolve	withwind	go round, wind
university	lorestead	seat of learning
vitreous	glassen	glass, glassy

4 False Etymology

Certain commentators have sought to discredit Barnes by pointing out that some of the words he invented contained Latin roots. Thus, for instance, for 'Chemistry' Barnes produced 'Matterlore'; 'matter' however does not come from Old English, but from Latin via French. Except in a very few cases we utterly reject this accusation. Although Barnes worked before the Oxford English Dictionary appeared (it was published two years after his death), let alone other now standard reference works on etymology, his own etymology was very rarely incorrect – indeed he was one of the great pioneers in the field. Thus Max Müller, who admired Barnes and came to visit him, was only just starting his linguistic investigations in Oxford. We cannot believe that Barnes was not aware, for example, of the etymology of 'matter'. Indeed the fact is that Barnes' neologisms or recommended replacement words often contained non-Old English roots. Thus among his new words we find, 'airfarer', 'airmeter', 'animal-lore', 'commonwealth', 'fablelore', 'mock-praise', 'rail-end', 'speech-tuning', 'stowcase', 'tooth-doctor' – all of which contain an English root and a Latin root. And we believe that Barnes was perfectly well aware of it. We would attribute this criticism of Barnes not to false etymology but to the academic's perfectionism. Barnes, though most learned, was not an academic. He did not conceive of an English language based on only English roots. As a linguist he well knew that other Germanic languages, including that closest to English, Frisian, borrowed freely from Latin. He also well knew that Old English itself had borrowings from Latin or Greek (for example, church, bishop, priest, school). Barnes did not want a fanatical linguistic purity, indeed he knew it was not possible – he could not himself find adequate substitutes for 'civilisation', 'river' or 'superstition'. What he wanted was a language where words of foreign origin would be dropped if fitting substitutes could be found or, alternatively if no substitute was available, foreign words could be assimilated. This is what he was advocating with words like 'matterlore' or 'toothdoctor'. Such words *sound* English, even if they are not wholly English. Barnes wanted a faithfulness to Saxon English, not necessarily in letter (since this was sometimes impossible) but *in spirit*. This is why he was quite happy to put forward 'masterpiece' as a replacement for 'chef d'oeuvre' or 'masterstroke' for 'coup de grâce'; though masterpiece consists of two words of Latin origin via French, it immediately *sounds* English – far more so than the purely French 'chef d'oeuvre'; the same is true for 'masterstroke'. With regard to this criticism of false etymology, let the academics put their dictionaries away and simply *listen*.

Praise

1 Barnes' Genius

The poetic genius of William Barnes, who saw through 'Englandish' to the soul of English, to its Old English 'Saxon' roots, found words of much loveliness and spiritual depth. His technique was first to define the essence of a thing and then find the words to express that essence. We greatly regret that words of his inspirational genius such as those that now follow have not been adopted into English speech:

English	Englandish	English	Englandish
backblaming	recrimination	play-tired	(of children in the evening)
becomesome	developmental	rimreach	circumference
fablelore	mythology	ringspell	encyclical
folkdom	democracy	safestead	asylum
homeborn	native	sleepstow	dormitory
horsethane	equerry	starfarer	astronaut
lightlore	optics	starhoard	constellation
lorecraft	erudition	starlore	astronomy
loreseeker	researcher	thought-theft	plagiarism
lorespeech	lecture	tidefleet	estuary
mendstead	prison	unhallow	desecrate
mindsight	imagination	wordcunning	sophistry
mock-praise	irony		

2 Logic

Barnes' genius was unique in being not only inspirational but also analytical. His approach to language was also the scientifically logical one of the philologist and etymologist. This means that, although Barnes is no longer physically alive, his system is and it can be continued. Thus from a substitute root-word, other words can readily be formed. Thus Barnes gives 'to wrangle' to replace 'to argue'. From this root the present author has formed: wrangler, wranglesome, wranglesomely, wranglesomeness, unwranglesome (arguer, argumentative, argumentatively, argumentativeness, conciliatory). In the same way from 'maysome' ('possible') we have unmaysome, maysomely, maysomeness, unmaysomeness, which we think that the reader will understand.

However we deem that we can go further than this and find new words, which Barnes himself never actually invented. Thus the present writer does not think that he has been unduly free in putting forward the following words, even though he has not found them in Barnes' works. He believes them to be in the spirit of Barnes:

Englandish	English	Englandish	English
air-force	airfleet	lecturer	lorespeaker
aristocracy	atheldom	lexicology	wordlore
astrology	starwrit	librarian	bookhoarder
bilingual	twyspeeched	modernise	benew
biology	lifelore	monetarism	geldlore
cassette-recorder	hearspell	patriotism	home-love
cautious	forewitsome	persuade	forsweeten
choreography	dancecraft	polytechnic	manycraftstead
computer	upthinker	prejudicial	foredeemsome
conscientious	inwitful	telephone	farspeaker
conurbation	town-cluster	television	farseer
dialogue	twayspeech	theology	Godlore
engineer	jinman	topography	steadlore
fallacious	flawsome	urbanise	betown
fax-machine	farprinter	video	seespell
information technology	spellcraftlore	video-cassette	seespellbox
inimical	foesome	videophone	seespeaker

The author thinks that other readers might be inspired to uncover other vocabulary in the same spirit. He has himself seen two shops in Barnes' own Wessex, one called 'Stitchcraft', selling sewing materials, and another called 'Timecraft', selling clocks, which make him think that there are indeed others like-minded who can add to Barnes' own word-hoard.

3 Triumph?

Very few of Barnes' neologisms actually found their way into the dictionary – one exception is bendsome, whose meaning is surely at once clear. However the writers of dictionaries do not count for much once a word is taken to the popular heart. Though long ignored by the compilers of dictionaries, 'skyline' is now commonplace and 'birdlore' is a usual enough replacement for the awkward 'ornithology'.

However, some of Barnes' successes have come among the English who emigrated. Freed of the constrictions of Establishment English, Anglo-Norman 'Englandish', those who emigrated, perhaps especially to 'New England', were free to use their own speech. Thus the English dialect 'fall' (of the leaf), 'gear', 'lonesome' and 'ongoing', now all common in the United States, were used by Barnes. Moreover, and this would surely delight Barnes, it is now common in North America to say 'mindset' and not 'mentality' and 'standout' and not 'exception'. Barnes would have appreciated 'sidewalk' and we have also heard 'sidewalker' – a good Saxon substitute for 'pedestrian'. The folk life of a younger people is giving utterance to Saxon English. Barnes would have been glad. Similarly, under American influence, we talk of a 'lone-parent' family rather than a 'monoparental' one (Barnes' idea – see Word-hoard) and 'people power' rather than 'democracy'. Admittedly the two elements in the latter compound are not English but they do *sound* English. The unharnessed energy of English abroad has given us expressions such as 'walkman', 'watchman' and the 'World Wide Web', the latter of which though resolutely modern, is all Old English alliteration and vocabulary. This 'New England/Old English' movement has also led to a partial denormanisation of spelling. Barnes was very much against the 'untruthful spelling' of English and would have approved of 'center' not 'centre', 'defense' not 'defence', 'inquire' not 'enquire', the latter of which Barnes foresaw in his 'inthrall' for 'enslave'.

This may look meagre, but Barnes' greatest vindication is not so much here, in the field of dialect words now become standard ones in at least one part of the English-speaking world, but elsewhere. It is firstly in the field of the phrasal verb (and noun). Both existed in the Victorian period but most were considered to be too vulgar to be used in literature. However, today, with the democratisation of literature and the literary language and its closeness to the spoken language, phrasal verbs and nouns have become innovative and fertile forms of language. Thus it would seem needless or even stuffy to use accept, demand, denigrate, despise, endorse, extinguish, persuade, produce and production when they can be replaced by take on, call for, run down, look down on, back up, put out, talk out off, turn out and output. In a similar way Latinate words, so popular in Victorian times, have indeed been replaced in many cases by English ones. The short (Anglo-Saxon) word is always preferable to the long (Latin) one. Thus we say not ameliorate, deteriorate, emphasise, environs, precursor, ramifications or vicinity, but rather better, worsen, highlight, outskirts, forerunner, ins and outs and neighbourhood. In this respect Barnes' most direct and successful heirs are the Plain English Campaign. And herein lies Barnes' ultimate victory – the triumph of *plain* English over complex and heavy Latinate English. It is a victory not of the exotic 'manqualm' or 'push-wainling' but a victory which is *plain* – fittingly discreet, almost unseen – like the man himself.

Barnes' critics might at least concede the above, but even so they would still no doubt continue to mock his more original neologisms. Who, they might ask is going to call a 'university' a 'lorestead' or a 'bus' a folkwain'? But perhaps all this is symbolically significant. Perhaps, after all, there are things in our modern world that are so ugly that they only deserve to be called by ugly and foreign words. They do not merit to bear Old English names. If the things themselves are spiritually foreign and ugly to us, then their names must also be spiritually foreign and ugly. It is no coincidence that one of the words that Barnes failed to English was 'civilisation'. He never managed to penetrate into the essence of the word and define its real meaning. Perhaps that is no surprise. When, some fifty years after Barnes' death, Gandhi was asked what he thought of Western civilisation, he replied that he 'thought it a good idea'. Perhaps the civilisation of the concentration camp, genocide, the Atom Bomb and ecological catastrophe simply does not deserve to be put into the fair speech of Old English.

Conclusions

Over forty years ago now the only linguist to study Barnes in earnest, Willis D. Jacobs, concluded his *William Barnes, Linguist* with these words: "Out of the sympathy of his heart and the conviction of his mind William Barnes presented the world with a number of revivified or devised terminologies which might serve in themselves, and as a model for others, to clarify education, help dissolve class snobbery, and reinvigorate the native genius of the English language. His work has been largely disregarded. His philological studies have been mostly ignored. With time, nevertheless, with continued research, the resources contained in Saxon English will be further revealed to the English-speaking world. The treasure will be great".

Over the years William Barnes has been much mocked for his neologisms. Many have pointed to the German Fascists and latter-day French chauvinists who have tried to nationalise their languages through force or legislation and of course failed. Languages are living and people will speak as they wish, no matter what the views of the political party in power or its law-making. Barnes, however, never forced his views on anyone, he merely put forward his ideas. And today another writer is doing for another language much that Barnes tried to do for English over a century ago. Just as Barnes worked to save English from the results of Normanisation, so today Alexander Solzhenitsyn is attempting to save the Russian language from the results of Sovietisation, by collecting obsolescent and dialect words which may still be used to replace Soviet Russian.

Such efforts may seem doomed to failure. Barnes himself was openly pessimistic and did not think that much would be achieved without a radical change of heart. For only a change of heart leads to a change of values and thus to a change of way of life and therefore speech. Efforts to save a language may be but a sigh before the end of the world but they may inspire the love of beauty. And that may in turn be just enough to inspire that very change of heart: the impossible is often the necessary.

Chapter 11

Word-Hoard

Barnes' neologisms have never been gathered together before. Although in *Early England and the Saxon-English* and *Speech-Craft*, he did actually give vocabulary lists, taken from a manuscript list, they were fairly short. Moreover many of Barnes' new words were used by him more or less unconsciously in his articles and books. The glossary that follows does not lay claim to being comprehensive – but it is certainly the most complete glossary so far put together. It is made up of both words he invented and alternative Standard English words he simply preferred to those of Latin origin. The latter (e.g. 'freedom' for 'liberty') are given even where they might seem obvious. A few technical words have been deliberately left out, being we thought of little interest (e.g. 'Linklessness' for 'Asyndeton' or 'Long sideling' for 'Amphimacrum'). The following list of over 1300 words could have been much longer had we included compound words. For instance the reader will find 'maysome' given as a substitute for 'possible', but he will not find the substitutes for 'possibly', 'possibility' 'impossible' or 'impossibility'. We are sure that, given the logic of Barnes' system, the reader who has read so far will be quite able to create those words, thus extending the word-hoard. Some readers may be surprised to see that no words are listed under the letters 'K', 'W' or 'Y'. This is for the simple reason that the vast majority of words beginning with those letters are Old English in origin in any case.

The following abbreviations are used:

adj.	adjective	gr.	grammar
alph.	alphabet	n.	noun
astr.	astronomy	ph.	philosophy
edu.	education	v.	verb
fin.	finance		

abandon	forgo, forsake	agglomerate (v.)	clodden
abject	downcast	agglutinate	upcleam
abnormal	odd, unshapely	agree with	hold with
absence	wantingness	aggressive	fightsome
absenteeism	absenteehood	agrarian	field
absolute	checkless	agriculture	fieldlore,
absolve	offloosen		earth-tillage,
absorb	forsoak, take in		earth-tilth
abstain	forbear	aimsome	single-minded
abstract	unmatterly	alienate	unfrienden
accelerate	onquicken,	allegory	forlikening
	quicken	alliteration	mate-penning
accent (gr.)	word-strain	allow	let
accept	intake	altercation	brangle, brawl
accessory (n.)	bykeeper,	altitude	height,
	deedmate		heightwiseness
accident	hapliness	ambassador	statespellsman
accidental	happensome	ambiguous	twymeaning,
accumulate	upheap, upgather		twysided
accusative (gr.)	end-case	ambush (v.)	lie in wait,
accustom	onwone		waylay
acephalous	headless	amicable	friendly
acoustics	sound-lore	amount	deal
acquaint	befriend	amphibious	two-aired, two-
across	athwart		breathed
action	deed	amplify	outbroaden
active	actsome,	amputate	forcarve
	doingsome,	anachronism	mistiming
	doughty, sprack	anagram	letter-shuffling
acute	high, sharp	analyse	forloosen
add	onput	ancestors	fore-elders,
adhere	oncleave		forebears,
adjective	thing mark-word		forefathers
adopt	intake	ancient	foreold
adorn	bedeck	anemometer	windmeter
adverb	under mark-word	animate	quicken
adversarial	thwartsome	annals	year-bookings
aeronaut	airfarer	annihilate	fornaughten
aesthetics	fairhoodcraft,	anniversary	yearday, yeartide
	fairhoodlore,	annoy	irk
	tastelore,	annoying	irksome
	tastecraft	annual	yearly
affectionate	lovesome	annuity	yeardole,
affirm	foraye		yeargyld

anodyne	pain-dilling, pain-dunting
anomalous	unwontsome
anticipate	forestall, fortake, forween
anticipation	forethought
antipenultimate	last but two
antique (adj.)	ereold, foreold
antithesis	withsetting, withstalling
apart	asunder
apathetic	listless
apogee (astr.)	earthoffing
appendix	onhenge
aphorism	thought-culling
apiary	beestead
apostrophe	offturning
apparent	seeming
appendix	onhenge
apprentice	underworker
aqueduct	waterlode
arbitrator	daysman
arboretum	treestow
archbishop	head-bishop
argue	wrangle
arithmetic	talecraft
armistice	weapon-staying
arrival	incoming
arson	forburning
art	craft
assimilate	forselfen
assizes	gemot
associate	fellow
association	fellowship
assume	so-take
asterisk	starkin
astonish	amaze
astronaut	starfarer
astronomy	starcraft, starlore
asylum	safestead
atmosphere	welkin-air
attentive	heedsome
attract	fordraw
au fait	ready-handed,

auction	thorough-skilled bidsale, bode-sale
audacious	(over)bold
audible	hearable
augment	forstrengthen, eke on, eke out
austere	tart
auxiliary (gr.n.)	bye-word
aviary	birdstead
avoid	sidestep, shun, shirk
balance (v.)	put straight
balanced	even-handed
barometer	airmeter
beautiful	comely, fair lovely
beauty	comeliness, fairhood, loveliness
bellicose	fightsome, warlike
belligerent	war-waging
benevolence	goodwill
bibulous	soaksome
bicycle	wheel-saddle
bilateral	two-sided
biography	lifewrit
biology	lifelore
botany	wortlore
braille	fingerspeech
burglary	housebreaking
butler	cellarthane
calculate	work out
cannibal	man-eater
capricious	self-willed
carnivorous	flesh-eatsome
carpenter	woodcraftsman
cause (v.)	bring about
cause (n.)	outcoming
caution	forewit
cavalry	horsemen
celestial	heavenly
cemetery	gravestead,

	licherest, burial-ground	concord	matching
century	yearhundred	concrete	matterly
chemistry	matterlore	conditional	straitened
chronology	timelore	conditional (gr.)	hinge-mood
chronometer	timemeter	condone	forlet, forsink
choose	pick (out)	conflict (n.)	strife
circular (n.)	touting-sheet	confuse	bemuddle
circumference	rimreach	congregate	upthrong
citizen	townsman, town-dweller	congress	loremote
		conjugate	forshapen
clarify	clearen	conjunction	link-word
clause	word-cluster	connected with	akin to
cognate	akin, kin	connection	link, bond
coherent	upcleaving	connoisseur	understander
coincide	fall in with	conscience	inwit
colic	bowel-wark	conscious	aware
collect	gather	consciously	wittingly, knowingly
collective	gathered, clustered	consider	look on as, deem
		console	cheer
collision	upclashing	consonant	breath-penning, clipping
colour	hue		
combination	bysetting	consort (n.)	lifemate
comfort	cheer	constellation	starhoard, starcluster
comic	light-hearted		
command	bid	construction	upbuilding
commandment	behest, bodeword, bidding	consummation	fullheighten-ing
		contaminate	befoulv
commerce	trade	contemporary	time-even, with the times
commiserate	overyearn	contempt	scorn
common	rife, widespread, wonted	continent (n.)	mainland
		continent (adj.)	forholding
complement	outfilling, upfilling,	continuity	ekeness
		continuous	ongoing
completely	fully, wholly	contract (v.)	updraw
compliant	yieldsome	contradict	gainsay
compose of	make up of	contradictory	gainsaying
composition	word-building	controversy	strife, wrangling
compound (gr.n.)	clustered word	convert (v.)	shift
concede	yield	convoy	fleetward
concert	gleemote	co-ordinate	rank-mate, row-mate
conchology	shell-lore		
conclusion	upshot	copious (speech)	wordrich, wordy

134

cordial	warm-hearted	demand (v.)	call for
corporal	bodily	demand (n.)	call
correct (adj.)	right	democracy	folkdom
corrode	rust	democratic	folkdomly
coterminous	even-ended	demonstrate	outshow
country	land	denigrate	slight
countrymen	landfolk	denote	bemark
coup de grâce	masterstroke	dentist	tooth-doctor
courageous	stout-hearted	deny	gainsay
course (edu.)	loreline	depend	hang on
cover (v.)	overspread	dependency	beholdingness
cowardly	faint-hearted	dependent	holding to
creator	maker	depict	outhue, outliken
crepuscule	evenglome	depilatory (n.)	hair-bane
criterion	redeship	depopulate	forwaste, unfolk
critic	deemster	deportment	behaviour
critical	deemsterly	deposit (fin.n.)	bewaring,
criticism	deemstery,		earnest,
	deemsterhood	deprave	forshrew, forwarp
cruel	hard-hearted,	depraved	wicked
	heartless, ruthless	depressed	downcast
culmination	uptippening	descendants	aftercomers
cultivate	till	descent	downsinking
curator	placewarden	describe	outmark
curriculum	loreway	description	outline
curtain	(fore)hanging	desecrate	unhallow
custom	wont	desert (n.)	wilderness
cygnet	swanlet	desist	forbear
dative (gr.)	to-case	desolate	forloned
decapitate	behead	desolation	forwasting
deciduous	leaf-shedding,	desperate	hopelorn
deciduous	fallsome	despise	look down on
decrease	lessen	destroy	fordo
defective	wanting	detain	hold (back)
deficiency	underodds	deter	forfray
defile	teamstrait	determine	offmark
define	formark	deteriorate	worsen
definite	formarked,	detestable	loathsome
	marksome	detrimental	harmful
dejected	downcast	develop	unfold, unroll
deliberate	wilful	developed	fledged
delight	mind-glee	developmental	becomesome
delude	mislead	devise	think up
demagogue	folk-leader	devour	eat up

devout	godly	distinguish	offmark, outshow
diagram	draught,	distract	draw away
	offdrawing	distribute	fordeal, outdeal,
dialect	folkspeech,		give out
	fortongueing,	disturbing	unsettling,
	homely speech,		upsetting
	sunderspeech	disyllabic	tway-sounded
diaphanous	throughshin-ing,	diversity	sundriness,
	through-showing		otherness
dictionary	wordbook	divisible	sundersome
didactic	teaching,	division	sundering
	teachsome	divorce	forsunder
difference	sundriness	domestic	housely, homely
different	sundry,	domicile	abode, wonestead
difficulty	hardship	dominant	uppermost
dilapidated	ramshackle	dormitory	sleepstow
diligence	earnestness	double (adj.)	twofold
diligent	toilsome	draper	clothmonger
diminish	lessen	dress (v.)	clothe
diminutive (n.)	forlessening	duplicate (adj.)	twayfold
diocese	bishopric	duty	business, task
diphthong	twysound	dynamics	mightcraftlore
direction	way	easily	readily
disadvantage	drawback	easy	ready
disastrous	baleful	eclipse (v.)	swarthen
discard	cast off, forcast	economic	sparesome
discourage	put off, daunt	edible	eatsome
discuss	talk over	educate	enlighten, school
disdain	scorn	education	schooling
dislike	mislike	effort	striving
dislocate	unstead	eject	outcast
dismiss	forsend	electric	matterquick
disperse	outsend	electricity	fireghost,
dispose	sunderset		matterquick-ness
dispute	wrangle	elevated	lofty
disrupt	forbreak, to-break	elicit	outdraw
disseminate	outscatter, outsow	eliminate	rid, cast out
dissidence	sunderthought	eloquent	telling, well-
dissident	sunderthinker		worded
dissimilar	unlike,	elucidate	forclear, outclear,
	unmatchsome		outshow
dissipate	forscatter	embassy	statespell
dissuade	offsweeten	emphasis	speech-strain
distance	way	emporium	cheapstow

embrasure	gun-gap	exclude	forclose, shut out,
encourage	cheer, take heart,		rule out
	quicken	exclusive	outshutsome
encyclical	ringspell	excrescence	outgrowth
enemy	foe, foeman	exegetical	outclearening
enlighten,	school	exhale	outbreathe
enslave	inthrall	exhibit	outshow
enthusiasm	faith-heat	exile (v.)	outban
entreat	beseech	exit	outgate
environs	outskirts	exodus	outfaring
epidemic	manqualm	expand	outbroaden,
episcopal	bishoply		outspread,
equality	evenhood		outstretch
equerry	horsethane	expatriate (v.)	outland
equilibrium	weight-eveness	expect	look out for
equinox	even-night	explain	clear up, set out,
equipment	gear		set forth expose,
equivalent	worth-eveness		put out
equivocal	twaysome	express	beword, utter,
error	mistake		word
erudite	learned	expressive	well-worded
erudition	lorecraft	extension	outspreading
erysipelas	wildfire	extortion	ravelock
especially	above all	extract (n.)	outculling
estuary	tidefleet	extreme	utmost
eternal	everlasting	extremely	most
ethnology	kincraftlore	exude	outooze
etymology	word-shapening	faculty	makingness
euphemism	fair-speaking,	fail	fall short of
	fair-wording	fallacious	unsound
euphony	sound-sweet,	fallacy	flaw
	well-	false	cheatsome,
	soundingness		guilesome, sham
evoke	call out	familiarity	upmating
exaggerate	greaten	family	kin, kinfolk
exaggerated	far-fetched	feminine (adj.)	womanly
exalt	forheighten	feminine (gr.)	quean sex
exceed	overgo	fertile	growsome
excellent	outstanding	file (of men)	man-team
except	out-take	filaceous	threaden
excess	overodds	finally	endly, lastly
excessive	passing	firm	steadfast
excessively	overly	flexible	bendsome
excite	raft	fluctuate	waver

focus	raymote	group	cluster
foliate (adj.)	leafen	halo	moon-trendle,
forceps	nipperlings,		sun-trendle
	tonglings	haughty	overmindy,
form (v.)	shapen		overmoody
formation	shapening	headquarters	highstead
formerly	hitherto	hepatitis	liver-sickness
fortress	stronghold	herbivorous	grass-eatsome
fossil	forestonening	hiatus	yawning
foundation	grounding,	hibernate	(over)winter,
	groundwork		winterwone
fragile	breaksome	hieroglyphics	sight-speech
fragments	brocks	horizon	skyedge, sky-line,
franchise (n.)	freedom		skysill
frank	forthright,	horrible	frightly,
	outspoken		frightening
fraternal	brotherly	human	menly
frugal	sparesome	humble (adj.)	lowly, lowly-
frustrate	thwart		minded, meek
future (adj.)	forthcoming	humble (v.)	meeken
future (n.)	aftertime,	hybrid	mongrel
future (n.)	hereafter	hydrophobia	water-awe
garrulous	talksome, wordy	hydrostatics	waterweight-lore
gay	blithesome	hyperbole	overcasting,
genealogy	kinlore		overshooting
generous	big-hearted,	hyphen	tie-stroke
	unstinting	hypothetical	so-put, idea,
generation	bairn-team, child-		thought
	team	identity	sameness
genitive (gr.)	offspring case	idiom	folkwording
genuflect	knee-bow	ignite	kindle
geography	earthwrit	ignorant	loreless
geology	earthlore	illegal	unlawful
globule	ballkin	illegible	unreadable
glory	brightness	illusory	guilesome
glossary	word-hoard,	imagination	mindsight
	wordlist,	immaculate	spotless,
	wordstore		unwemmed
glossarist	word-culler	immediate	forthwith
grammar	speechcraft	immediately	at once
grandiloquent	high-talking	immortal	deathless
grateful	bethanksome,	impart to	bestow on
	thankful	impend	overhang
gratuitous	out of kindness	imperative (gr.)	bidding word

138

impersonal	deederless, thingnameless	interest (n.)	care
		interest (fin.)	loan-meed
impertinence	meddlesomeness	interfering	meddlesome
impetuous	headstrong, (over)hasty	internally	inly
		international	worldwide
implore	beseech	interpolate	infoist
importance	weight	interrupt	break in, cut in
imposed	put upon	intimidating	daunting
incandescent	white-hot	intolerable	unbearable
incantation	spell	introduce	bring in
incarnate	embody	inundate	beflood
incidence	onfall	invade	overrun
inclination	bent (of mind)	invasion	inroad
inconvenient	unhandy	invalid (adj.)	unhale
incorporate	embody	invective	inwaging
increase	swell	invent	think up
incredible	unbelievable	invert	end-shift
incur	run up	inveterate	unoldened
indebted	beholden	invisible	unseen
indecent	unseemly	irony	mock-praise
indicate	mark, mark-word	irritate	irk
indicative (gr.)	surehood	irritating	irksome
individuality	oneness	isolate	cut off
induction (ph.)	law-tracking	issue (v.)	give forth
industrious	toilsome, worksome	joyful	blithesome
		judge (v.)	deem
ineffable	untellable	judge (n.)	deemer
inferior	lower	judgement	doom
inhabit	dwell, live	jurisprudence	lawcraft
inhale	inbreathe	just	fair
iniquitous	wrongwise	juvenile	youthful
injure	wrong, hurt	laboratory	workstead
initial (n.)	word-head	laborious	toilsome
innocent	childlike	labour	toil
insect	incarveling	laburnum	golden chain
insensitive	feelingless, thin-skinned	labyrinth	maze
		language	speech, tongue
insist	stand to	lapidary (n.)	gem-cutter, gem-shaper
instinct	ongoading		
instruction	loredom	latitude	breadthwiseness
intelligence	wit(s)	laxative	loosensome
intelligent	quick-witted, sharp-witted	lecture	lorespeech
		legal	lawful
interest (v.)	becare	legible	readable

139

letter (alph.)	speech-token	medicine	leechcraft
leveret	hareling	mediocre	middling
lexicology	wordlore	melancholy	heavy-hearted
liberal	free-minded	mellifluent	honeysweet
liberalise	unfetter,	menace (v.)	threaten
	unshackle	menagerie	animalstead
liberty	freedom	mental	mindly
library	bookhoard	mention (v.)	foreset
lieutenant	steadholder	merchant	chapman
lieutenancy	steadholder-hood	merciful	mildhearted
limit	bound	message	byspell
liquidate	offclear	metallic	metallen
literature	booklore	metaphorical	overcarrying
lithography	stone-printing	meteor	welkin-fire
locative (gr.)	stowcase,	meteorology	weatherlore
	steadcase	metonymy	name-changing
locomotive (adj.)	steadgoing	microscope	closeseer
locomotion	onfaring	misfortune	mishap
logic	redecraft,	mitigate	milden
	redelore	modest	shamefast
logician	redesman	modify	mould
longitude	lengthwiseness	modulation	speech-tuning
longitudinal	longwise	mollify	soften
loyal	true-hearted	monitor (n.)	warner
lucid	clear-sighted	monody	lonesong
lunatic	moonmad,	monologue	lonespeech
	moonsick	monopolise	lonebuy
machine	ginny, jinny	monopoly	lonesale
magnanimous	great-minded	monosyllable	breath-sound
magnificent	high-deedy, high-	monosyllabic	onesounded
	doing, lordly	monotony	lonesound
magnify	greaten	mournful	moansome
maintain	uphold, keep up	multiple	manifold
manual (n.)	handbook	murder	slay
manuscript	handwrit	music	gleecraft
maritime	sea-edged, sea-	musician	gleeman
	skirting	mutton	sheepmeat
marriage	wedlock	mythology	fablelore
masculine	manly	naive	artless
masculine (gr.)	carl sex	native	homeborn
maternal	motherly	navigation	seafaring
mathematics	rimecraft	navy	fleet
matterly	concrete	naysome	negative
mechanics	mattermight	necessary	needsome

negate	fornay	ornithology	birdlore
negative	fornaysome	orthodox	right-minded
neglect	forlet, overlook	osteology	bonelore
negligent	unheedsome	outmoded	behind the times
negotiations	talks	palace	thronestead
neuter	unsexly	pale	wan
noble	lofty-thoughted, well-born	palpitate	throb
		panacea	allheal
nomenclature	benaming, name-shapening	parade	offshowing
		paragraph	offwriting, wording-share
nominative (gr.)	of-spoken case		
nonentity	nothingness	parapet	folkward
notion	thought	paraphrase	new bewording
noticeable	markworthy	parliament	witan
noun	name-word, thing-name, thing-word	parody	song-mocking
		part	deal, share
		participate	take part
number	tale	particle (gr.)	wordling
obedient	hearsome	particular	sharesome
object (gr.)	speech-matter	partner	mate
objective (adj.)	outwoning	party	mirthmote
obliged	beholden	passive (gr.)	time-giving
oblique	slanting	past (n.)	foretime, heretofore
obsolete	outwonted		
obstacle	hindrance	paternal	fatherly
obstruct	hamper, hinder	patronymic	sire-name
obstructive	hindersome	pathology	painlore
occasion	time	peculation	thefting
occurrence	happening	pedal	footkey
ointment	salve	pedigree	kinstem
old-fashioned	old-world	penultimate	last but one
omit	outleave	people	folk
omen	foretoken	perambulator	push-wainling
omnibus	folkwain	perceive	fortake
omnipotent	almighty	percolate	forstrain
onomatopoeia	mocking name	perfect (adj.)	fordone, forended, outbuilt, outshapen
operation	working		
oppose	set against		
opposite (adj.)	overthwartsome		
opposition	overthwarting	perjure	forswear
optics	lightlore	permanent	settled
oration	rede-speech	permit (v.)	let
orbit	path-bow	pernicious	baneful
origin	stem	persecute	hound

persevere	outstand	precious	dearworth
perverse	froward,	precursor	forerunner
	wayward, wrong-	predestination	foredooming
	headed	predict	foretell
pervious	throughletting	preface	forenote, foresay,
petrify	(for)stonen		foreword
philology	speechlore	prefer	would rather,
phobia	awe		would sooner
phonetic	soundly	prefix	fore-eking,
photograph	sunprint		forewordling,
phrase	word-cluster,		word-heading
	wordset	pregnant	with child
physical	bodily	prejudice (n.)	foredeeming
physiology	naturelore	premise (ph.)	forestep
pillage	ransack	premonition	forefeeling
pious	godly	preponderate	overweigh
pirate	searobber, sea-	preposition	case-word,
	rover		foreputting
piston	plunger	present (adj.)	now
place	spot, stead, stow	present (n.)	gift
plagiarism	thought-theft	presentiment	forefeeling
plant	wort	prevent	stay
playful	playsome	priority	forehood
pleasant	winsome	prison	mendstead
pleonasm	overfilling of	probability	likelihood,
	speech		mightsomeness
pleurisy	side-addle	proceed to	forthgo
plural	manysome,	procession	teamgang
	somely	professor	lorefather
pneumatics	airlore	profound	deep
poem	lay	programme	foredraught
political economy	governlore	progress	headway
polygamist	manywedder	prologue	forespeech
polyglot (adj.)	manyspeeched	pronoun	stead-word,
polytheism	manygodhood		name-token
popular	folk	pronounce	breathpen
portent	foretoken	proposition (ph.)	outwording,
portray	outhue, outliken		thought-putting
positive	ayesome	property (ph.)	selfliness
possible	maysome	proprietor	householder,
possessed	devilsick,		owner
	fiendsick	prospect	outlook
posterity	afterkin	prosperous	wealth-owning
potential	mayly	protect	ward

protégé	ward	relative	kinsman,
prototype	forepattern,		kinswoman
	foreshape	relative (adj.)	slight
prove	trow	release	let go, let out
proverb	byword, saying	relieve	soothe
provoke	bring about, call	religion	faith-law
	forth	religious	withholden
prudence	forewit	remember	bear/keep in
punctuate	bestop		mind, recall
pure	clean, sheer	remote	outstep
purify	cleanse	remove	take away
pursue	follow	rendezvous	meetingstead
pusillanimous	weak-minded	renounce	forego, give up
quadrangle	fourwinkle	repeat	say again
quadruple	fourfold	replace	take the stead
quality	suchness	representative	steadsman
quantity	muchness	repress	quell, underhold
quarrel (v.)	fall out	reprimand (v.)	upbraid
question	asking	republic	commonwealth
race	kin	researcher	loreseeker
railings	folkscreen	resemblance	likeness
rapid	swift	reserve	misgiving
ravage	lay waste	reservoir	watergiver
reason	ground	reside	dwell, live
reasoning	redeship	residence	abode, wonestead
rebel (v.)	rise up	resist	stand up to,
recently	lately, latterly, of		withstand
	late	resistant	withstandsome
recover	uphalen	responsible	answerable
recrimination	backblaming	restrain	inhold, forhold
recalcitrant	withspurring	restrict	instraiten, stint
rectify	righten, straighten	restricted	bounded,
	out		straitened
reduce	bring down,	result	backspring,
	lessen		outcome,
refer to	think of		outworking,
reflection	backshine		upshot
refrain	offhold	resume	take up again
regency	regenthood	resurrection	rising again,
regret	rankle, rue		uprising
reject	cast aside	retain	hold back,
related	beholden		withhold
relation	beholdeness,	reticent	tongue-tied,
	dealing, kinship		tongue-tying

retire	withdraw	sincere	heartfelt
revenue	income	singular	onely, onesome
revolt (v.)	rise up	size	bigness
revolve	withwind	slavery	thraldom
rhetoric	redecraft, rede-speech	society (group)	club
		solecism	miswording
rich	wealthy	solid	staunch
ridiculous	laughable	solidarity	byholdingness
river	main-stream	solstice	sunsted
royal	kingly	sophist	wordwise
royalty	kinghood	sophistry	rede-cunning,
rumour	hearsay		rede-guile,
rural	landly		word-cunning
salubrious	halesome, healthy, wholesome	soporific (adj.)	sleepgiving
		sort	kind
		souvenir	keepsake
satisfaction	happiness	species	hue
school	lorehouse	spiral (adj.)	withwinding
sciatica	hip-wark	spiritual	ghostly
science	lore, skill	spiritual art	soul painting
scientific	lore	spiritual vision	soulsight
scintillate	sparkle	spirituality	ghosthood
secular	worldly	stable	steadfast
selective	choosy	statics	weightcraft-lore
semi-detached	twin	stereotype	block-type
sense	redeship	stimulate	upgoad,
sensitive	thin-skinned		upquicken
sentence (gr.)	thought-wording	store	hoard
separate (v.)	offsunder	strict	stern
separable	sundersome	study (n.)	lore
serious	earnest	stupid	dull-witted, slow-witted
sermon	lorespell		
servant	thane	subdivision	undershare
serve	see to	subject (gr.n.)	fore-end, speech-thing
servile	craven		
session	sitting	subject (v.)	underhold
severe	harsh	subjective	inwoning
sign	token	subjunctive (gr.)	hinge-mood
signify	betoken	submarine (adj.)	undersea
silent	unuttered	sub-species	underhue
similar	akin to	substance	being
similarity	likeness	substantial	sound
similarly	likewise	substitute (n.)	steadman
simple	homespun	subtend	underspan

subterfuge	underslinking	telegram	wire-spell
subterranean	underground	telegraph	spell-wire
subtract	take away	telescope	spyglass
succumb	fall to	temperate	forholding
suffering	hardship	tense (gr.)	time-shape,
suffix	end-eking,		timing
	on-eking,	terminate	end
	mark-ending,	terminology	wording
	word-ending	terminus	rail-end
suitability	fitness	thatched	thatchen
suitable	fitting	topography	placewrit
superannuated	overyeared	transfer	shift
supercilious	brow-knitting,	transitive	overfaresome
	overweening	transitive (gr.)	outreaching
supereminent	overtippening	translate	put into,
superficial	shallow	transparent	through-showing
superior	higher	travel	fare
superlative	highest pitch	traveller	wayfarer
superpose	overlay	treaty	bargain
superstition	idle belief	tributary	side-stream
supervise	overwatch	trinity	threeness
supplicate	undercrave	triple	threefold
suppose	so-take	type	kind
supremacy	elderdom,	typhus	lent-addle
	eldership,	typographer	printer
	headship,	ultimate	yonder
	upper hand	unabated	unlessened
surpass	overgo	uneducated	unschooled
surprise (v.)	take aback	unfortunate	ill-starred,
surrender	give in		luckless
survive	outlive	uninteresting	of no odds
syllable	breath-sound	unity	oneness
sympathise	feel with	universal	allsome
synonymous	wordsame	university	lorestead, seat of
synonym	mateword,		learning
	namesame	unlimited	unbounded,
syntax	speech-trimming,	unlimited	unstinted
	speech-wording	unnecessary	needless
tacit	unspoken,	unusual	unwonted
	wordless	used to	wont to
tactics	warlore	useful	handy
tautology	word-sameness	useless	unhandy
technical	artly, craftly	usual	wonted
tedious	longsome	up to date	with the times

vague	dim
vain	idle
valid	true
variegated	many-hued
variety	sundriness
various	sundry
ventilator	airgiver
veracious	soothfast
verb	time-word
very	highly, most
vibrate	whiver
vicinity	neighbourhood
view	outlook
vigilant	wakeful, watchful
virgin	unwedded
virile	manly
visible	seen
vision	sight
vocabulary	word-hoard, wordlist, wordstore
vocation	calling
vocative (gr.)	call-case
voluntary	wilful
voracious	greedy
vowel	breathsound
vulgar	low, low-minded
zoology	animal-lore

Conclusion

To say that we shall never see his like again would be to prophesy when we do not know, a proceeding proverbially unwise; but I do think that it may well be the ambition of us all, when our time shall come, to have lived as Mr. Barnes lived and to have died as he died.

Rev. O. P. Cambridge, 'In Memoriam', p.xxvii

Very tender, very true, is the last song of the old Saxon minstrel.

From a newspaper report in Scrapbook II, p.34

'Some men live before their age, others behind it. My father did both. In action he was behind the world, or rather apart from it; in thought he was far before his time – a thinker who may probably lead the next generations even more than his own. A great and deep student of the past, he drew from it inferences and teaching for the future'.[183]

As a man of both the past and the future, Barnes was both traditional and radical, or perhaps radical because traditional and traditional because radical. His deep, compassionate and original mind went to the roots and inner meanings of all things, in Religion, Nature, Art, Marriage, Society, Economics, Politics and Language. He sought to find what lay behind apparent reality with all its injustices and distortions and to penetrate to the ultimate truths and origins of things. He held real beliefs and values, neither ambitions nor conventions – as can be seen from his ignoring of fashion in his way of dressing. His mind was too original to work within the constraints of parties, systems and ideologies. The only system or ideology of this heavenly-minded man was the spiritual and moral beauty of the Gospels, of 'Christian kindness', no system or ideology at all, but a way of life. And it was this that he defended, a way of life, that of

---

[183] Baxter, Preface

England's Saxon peasantry, that of his childhood, that of Paradise. This was his vision.

Barnes kept faith with the England that had gone before him. Thus the people of his time, in the heat of Victorian 'Progress' would not accept him, not because he was wrong but because they were not spiritually ready for him. Since then William Barnes has been mocked by many who have not kept faith with the past, the old traditions of English life. But those who have mocked him are among those who have no way out of the present dead end. As a believer, Barnes never spoke their language of cynicism and to them he might have uttered the very words of one of his sermons: 'Men with knowledge are often foolish'.[184] Supposing Barnes, after all, saw true? And suppose there is something prophetic in him, that this pre-industrial man has something to say to our post-industrial society? Our age may yet be more receptive to his values.

Since he lived in the past and the future, we cannot agree with one of his admirers who called him 'the last of the believers',[185] for his future has become our present. Therefore we see him rather as a forerunner from the past, and we would rather call him '*the first of the believers*'. Many-skilled, he was a complete man: 'During his long and arduous life William Barnes used every single talent his Master had entrusted to him'.[186] He held that man was a unity of body, mind and soul and that his physical, mental and spiritual needs were to be met. He both preached and practised this ideal of the complete man, of wholeness and integrity. He held the same Trinitarian ideal as the monk, who is to share his time between manual work, mental activity and prayerful worship.

In the Middle Ages we can suppose that William Barnes would have been Roman Catholic. In the nineteenth century he was an Anglican country priest. At the end of the twentieth century we might wonder

---

[184] Sermon at Came 27 August 1876
[185] Llewellyn Powys, *Dorset Essays*, 'The Grave of William Barnes', London 1935, p.29
[186] Dugdale, pp.232-3

where he would belong. In 1986 a speaker at the William Barnes Society said: 'The Church of England is an institution Barnes would barely recognise'.[187] Indeed, Barnes himself was an admirer of the Old English Church: 'The Saxon-English Church, although she was a branch of the Church of Rome, did not hold – what, indeed, the mother-church had not then broached – all the doctrines which our Church cast off at the Reformation as unsound and not of Catholic truth'.[188] At the beginning of the third millennium, Barnes' radical and traditional orthodox Christianity would surely have led him elsewhere to seek spiritual values and nourishment.

Over a century has passed since William Barnes' death. Since his times World Wars have come, Empire has gone, United Kingdom and Europe have come – and tomorrow they in turn will be gone. And as the new millennium approaches we may think of Shakespeare's words: 'What's to come is still unsure'. We are physically much more comfortable since William Barnes was amongst us, but at what cost? England today has lost beauty, it is, as Barnes would have had it, all 'glorylorn'. As he wrote:

> For aught that's nice You pay a price...
> To buy new gold Give up some old.[189]

Part of this price has been the loss of roots, not only here but in many parts of the world, as others too pass through the same processes as ourselves: 'The tale is important because the history of this small island off the shore of Europe became world history, its speech became world speech, and, perhaps more important, its social and economic experience also became that of the rest of the world'.[190] 'It may be that in these troubled times that William Barnes will at last come into his own as the much needed philosopher and friend of the

---

[187] Mr. C. H. Sisson in *Proceedings of the William Barnes Society* 1983–92, vol.I, p.94

[188] *Early England and the Saxon English*, p.85

[189] William Barnes, *The Cost of Improvement*

[190] *Domesday A Search for the Roots of England*, Michael Wood 1986, BBC Publications.

people of many lands, creeds and languages'.[191] As we go into a new millennium, his gleanings in so many fields may yet guide us in today's restless and rootless world, throwing light on future paths for our country.

Barnes is a forerunner. It is our belief that this idyllic poet, with his angelic mind and 'true and loving heart', this 'half-hermit, half-enchanter' has answers to many of the questions which trouble us today. He found, already in the nineteenth century, roots. He found those roots of England and English in their past, in Old England and Old English. He saw through the veneer of his own time to Saxon England; in 'soulsight' he saw Alfred at Winchester and Edward at Corfe. He wanted the rebirth of not just Saxon English but also Saxon England and its whole civilisation of chesters and minsters, lying like a white stone in the English collective memory. In other words he envisioned the denormanisation of England and English and, through that, the spiritual rebirth of England and English. Although for Barnes, as for us, the Norman Conquest had taken place physically, for him it had not taken place spiritually, for in his soul he lived both before it and in a continuing Old England of the present. And this is William Barnes' England. For Barnes' voice is the voice of Old England.

Since we began the Conclusion to this book with the first words from Lucy Baxter's biography of her father, perhaps we can do no better than end it with her last words which quote Professor Palgrave's description of her father's funeral and her own thought of her beloved father:[192]

'I was again before the gate leading down to the little rectory, deep amongst trees as yet untouched by autumn. There I saw the plain elm coffin carried out and placed on a little hand-bier, covered only by many wreaths and crosses of white, spring-like flowers; then drawn forth and followed by a little crowd of the poet's children and grandchildren. In company with many friends and neighbours –

---

[191] Hinchy, p.72
[192] Baxter, p.326–7

words which in his case were identical – I followed to his own gray little church, where with the sweet, solemn words which he had himself read over old and young, and the nosegays of cottage flowers which the children shyly dropped into his grave, in the 'sure and certain Christian hope, he was laid to rest from his labours'.

But not dead – the true poet can never die'.

Select Bibliography

The best Bibliography (15 pages in length) of works by or on Barnes is to be found in Trevor Hearl's excellent *William Barnes the Schoolmaster*. There also exists a very useful 'Catalogue of the Works by and about William Barnes in Dorchester Reference Library'. The present short Bibliography lists only writings relevant to this work and therefore gives only a modest idea of the huge range of William Barnes' interests. In Section One the reader will find a list of books, articles, letters and manuscripts written by Barnes which have been quoted from or mentioned in this work. In Section Two he will find, in addition to a list of major editions of Barnes' poetry published since his death, a list of books and articles written on Barnes which have been quoted from or mentioned here. All poems quoted in this work have been taken from the two-volume edition of Barnes' poetry edited by Bernard Jones. All works referenced 'London' were published by John Russell Smith, unless otherwise stated.

Section One: Works by William Barnes

a) *Manuscript Material*

The Dorset County Museum contains the Barnes Archive, with a copy of all his published works and also ten cartons of his manuscript sermons, seven scrapbooks (now on microfilm), his diary (with translation from Italian), eight exercise books of poems, correspondence, MS articles, sketches, notes, pamphlets and newspaper cuttings.

b) *Selected Published Material*

1820 Poetical Pieces, Dorchester.

1822 Orra, A Lapland Tale, Dorchester.

1827 Linguiana (Signed Dilettante), Dorset County Chronicle (DCC), 6, 13 and 20 December.

1829 The Etymological Glossary, Shaftesbury and London , J. Rutter.

1830 'Corruptions of the English Language', *Gentleman's Magazine* (*GM*) June, pp.501–3. 'Leniency to Criminals: Thieves and Punishment', *DCC*, 2 September. 'Formation of English Compounds', *GM* November, pp.393–6.

1831 'On English Derivatives', *GM* June, p.500.

1832 'On Compounds in the English Language', *GM* Supp.Vol.CII, pp.590–3

1833 'Formation of the English Language', *GM* Supp.Vol.CIII, pp.591-2.

1840 'The Saxon Dialect of Dorsetshire', *GM* January, pp.31–3. *An Investigation of the Laws of Case in Language*, London, Longman & Co.

1841 'Education in Words and in Things', *GM* January p.22.

1842 *The Elements of English Grammar*, London, Longman and Co.

1844 'On Harmonic Proportion Applied to Churches', *GM* February, p.136. *Sabbath Lays, Six Sacred Songs*, London, F. W. Smith. *Poems of Rural Life, in the Dorset Dialect: With a Dissertation and Glossary*, London. (Other editions in 1847, 1862 and 1866).

1846 *Poems, Partly of Rural Life (in National English)*, London.

1848 'Humilis Domus', *Poole and Dorset Herald*, 12 April to 24 May

1849 'Se Gefylsta' ('The Helper'): *An Anglo-Saxon Delectus*, London. 1854 *A Philological Grammar*, London.

1855 'Picture Frames', *The Art Journal* 12 February, pp.55–6.

1858 *Notes on Ancient Britain and the Britons*, London.

1859 *Views of Labour and Gold*, London.

1859 *Hwomely Rhymes*. A second collection of Poems in the Dorset Dialect, London. (Other editions in 1863 and 1864).

1861 Thoughts on Beauty and Art. *Macmillan's Magazine*, Vol.IV, pp. 126-37.

1862 *TIW; or, A View of the Roots and Stems of the English as a Teutonic Tongue*, London. *Poems of Rural life in the Dorset Dialect*, London. (Second edition in 1869).

1863 *A Grammar and Glossary of the Dorset Dialect*, Berlin, A. Asher and Co.

1864 Saxon-English History, *The Reader* 23 July, p.98.

1866 'A View of Christian Marriage', *The Ladies' Treasury* February-June, pp.82, 136, 195, 259, 327.

1866 'On the Welsh Triads', *Fraser's Magazine* October, pp. 536–44. 'Plagiarism and Coincidence; or thought-thievery and thought-likeness', *Macmillan's Magazine* November, pp.73–80.

1867 'Origin of Mankind', *The Hawk*, pp.298–303.

1868 *Poems of Rural Life in Common English*, London, Macmillan and Co.

1869 *Early England and the Saxon-English*, London. 'Written Evidence to the Government Commission on the Employment of Children, Young Persons and Women in Agriculture', Blue Book, Appendix Part II to the second report, pp.12–14.

1874 'Ealdhelm, First Bishop of Sherborne, Somerset' *Archaeological and Natural History Society Transactions* Vol.XX, pp.85–97.

1878 *An Outline of English Speech-Craft*, London, C. Kegan Paul and Co.

1879 *Poems of Rural Life in the Dorset Dialect*, London C. Kegan Paul and Co. (Later editions in 1883, 1887, 1888, 1893, 1898, 1902, 1905).

1880 *An Outline of Rede-Craft (Logic) with English wording*, London, C. Kegan Paul and Co.

1886 *A Glossary of the Dorset Dialect*, London, Trübner and Co.

Section Two: Works on William Barnes and Major Editions of His Poetry Since His Death

[An asterisk indicates that at the time of going to press the particular work was still in print and available at the Dorset County Museum bookshop or elsewhere].

1887 *The Life of William Barnes Poet and Philologist*, Lucy Baxter (Leader Scott), London, Macmillan.

1887 'In Memoriam'. Proceedings of Dorset Natural History and Anti-quarian Field Club, Rev. O. P. Cambridge, pp.xv-xxxiii.

1908 *Selected Poems of William Barnes* with notes by Thomas Hardy, Oxford.

1946 *The Mint*, Geoffrey Grigson, London, Routledge.

1948 *William Barnes. A Study of the Man and the Poet*, J. V. Ruffell, Ph.D. thesis, University of London.

1949 *Poems Grave and Gay*, Giles Dugdale, Dorchester, Longmans. 1950 *Selected Poems of William Barnes*, Geoffrey Grigson, London, Routledge and Kegan Paul.

1952 *William Barnes, Linguist*, Willis D. Jacobs, Albuquerque, University of New Mexico Press.

1953 *William Barnes of Dorset*, Giles Dugdale, London, Cassell.

1959 'A Word-hoard for Folkdom', Willis D. Jacobs, *Arizona Quarterly*, Summer 1959, 15, pp.157–61.

1960 *William Barnes, the Man and the Poems*, William Turner Levy, Dorchester, Longmans.

1962 *The Poems of William Barnes*, Bernard Jones, London, Centaur Press. (The definitive edition of Barnes' Poetry).

1963 'The Conserving Myth of William Barnes', R. A. Forsyth, *Victorian Studies 6*, pp.325–354.

1966 *The Dorset William Barnes*, Florence S. Hinchy, Blandford, Dorset Bookshop.

1966 *William Barnes The Schoolmaster*, Trevor W. Hearl, Dorchester, Friary Press.*

1971 *One Hundred Poems*: with an essay 'William Barnes' by E. M. Forster, Blandford, Dorset Bookshop.

1972 *William Barnes A Selection of His Poems*, Robert Nye.

1977 *Victorian Country Parsons* (William Barnes: Chapter 7), Brenda Colloms, London, Constable. 'William Barnes and the Social Problem', Chris Wrigley, Proceedings of the Dorset Natural History and Archaeological Society, pp.19–27.

1978 *William Barnes, Poems Grave and Gay,* reprint of a 1972 re-issue of the 1949 edition with a Foreword and Afterword by Alan Chedzoy, Weymouth, Weymouth Bookshop.*

1979 *Some Versions of Paradise: An Examination of Motive in the Poetry and Prose of William Barnes.* Mary Keane, Ph.D. thesis, Dalhousie.

1984 *William Barnes the Dorset Poet*, Chris Wrigley.*

1985 *William Barnes A Life of the Dorset Poet*, Alan Chedzoy, The Dovecote Press, Stanbridge, Wimborne, Dorset.*

1986 A Catalogue of Works By and About William Barnes in Dorchester Reference Library, Jennifer C. Ward, Dorset County Library.*

1993 Proceedings of the William Barnes Society 1983–92, Dorchester.*

1994 *William Barnes, Selected Poems*, Andrew Motion, Penguin.*

1996 *Collected Prose Works of William Barnes*, (in 6 vols.), Routledge.*

About the Author

The author, born in Essex in 1956, attended Colchester Royal Grammar School, going on to study Modern Languages at Oxford. Married with six children, he is an Orthodox priest and also teaches at the ESSEC Graduate School of Management in France. His previous books include *Orthodox Christianity and the Old English Church, The Hallowing of England* and *Orthodox Christianity and the English Tradition.*

Some of our other titles

see www.asbooks.co.uk for latest titles and prices

An Introduction to the Old English Language and its Literature
Stephen Pollington

The purpose of this general introduction to Old English is not to deal with the teaching of Old English but to dispel some misconceptions about the language and to give an outline of its structure and its literature. Here you will find an outline of the origins of the English language and its early literature. Such knowledge is essential to an understanding of the early period of English history and the present form of the language. This revised and expanded edition provides a useful guide for those contemplating embarking on a linguistic journey.

£5.95

First Steps in Old English
An easy to follow language course for the beginner
Stephen Pollington

A complete and easy to use Old English language course that contains all the exercises and texts needed to learn Old English. This course has been designed to be of help to a wide range of students, from those who are teaching themselves at home, to undergraduates who are learning Old English as part of their English degree course. The author has adopted a step-by-step approach that enables students of differing abilities to advance at their own pace. The course includes practice and translation exercises, a glossary of the words used in the course, and many Old English texts, including the *Battle of Brunanburh* and *Battle of Maldon*.

£16-95

Old English Poems, Prose & Lessons   2CD s
read by Stephen Pollington

This CD contains lessons and texts from *First Steps in Old English*.
Tracks include: 1. Deor. 2. Beowulf – The Funeral of Scyld Scefing. 3. Engla Tocyme (The Arrival of the English). 4. Ines Domas. Two Extracts from the Laws of King Ine. 5. Deniga Hergung (The Danes' Harrying) Anglo-Saxon Chronicle Entry AD997. 6. Durham 7. The Ordeal (Be ðon ðe ordales weddigaþ) 8. Wið Dweorh (Against a Dwarf) 9. Wið Wennum (Against Wens) 10. Wið Wæterælfadle (Against Waterelf Sickness) 11. The Nine Herbs Charm 12. Læcedomas (Leechdoms) 13. Beowulf's Greeting 14. The Battle of Brunanburh There is a Guide to Pronunciation and sixteen Reading Exercises

£15 2CDs - Free Old English transcript from www.asbooks.co.uk.

Learn Old English with Leofwin
Matt Love

This is a new approach to learning old English – as a *living language*. Leofwin and his family are your guides through six lively, entertaining, topic-based units. New vocabulary and grammar are presented in context, step by step, so that younger readers and non-language specialists can feel engaged rather than intimidated. The author has complemented the text with a wealth of illustrations. There are listening, speaking, reading and writing exercises throughout. Free soundtracks available on the Anglo-Saxon Books website.

£16.95 160 pages

Wordcraft   Concise English/Old English Dictionary and Thesaurus
Stephen Pollington
Wordcraft provides Old English equivalents to the commoner modern words in both dictionary and thesaurus formats. The Thesaurus presents vocabulary relevant to a wide range of individual topics in alphabetical lists, thus making it easily accessible to those with specific areas of interest. Each thematic listing is encoded for cross-reference from the Dictionary.

The two sections will be of invaluable assistance to students of the language, as well as those with either a general or a specific interest in the Anglo-Saxon period.

£9.95

Plain English – A Wealth of Words
Bryan Evans
Plain English has its roots in the language spoken by the English 1000 years ago. It is a beautiful language which fosters clear thought and speech. It is a language for those who like to say much with few words.

This wordbook outlines the story of English then it offers 'A hundred words to start you off' (*shorten* rather than *abbreviate*, *speed up* instead of *accelerate*, *drive home* rather than *emphasize*, and so on). In the main part of the book will be found over 10,000 English words that are still alive and well, then a list of some 3,600 borrowed words, with suggestions about English words we might use instead. It is hoped that this book will help readers think about the words they use, and in doing so speak and write more clearly.

£9.95   328 pages

Leechcraft: Early English Charms, Plantlore and Healing
Stephen Pollington
An unequalled examination of every aspect of early English healing, including the use of plants, amulets, charms, and prayer. Other topics covered include Anglo-Saxon witchcraft; tree-lore; gods, elves and dwarves.

The author has brought together a wide range of evidence for the English healing tradition, and presented it in a clear and readable manner. The extensive 2,000-entry index makes it possible for the reader to quickly find specific information.

The three key Old English texts are reproduced in full, accompanied by new translations.
Bald's Third Leechbook; *Lacnunga*; *Old English Herbarium*.

£25   28 illustrations   536 pages

A Guide to Late Anglo-Saxon England
From Alfred to Eadgar II 871–1074
Donald Henson
This guide has been prepared with the aim of providing the general readers with both an overview of the period and a wealth of background information. Facts and figures are presented in a way that makes this a useful reference handbook.

Contents include: The Origins of England; Physical Geography; Human Geography; English Society; Government and Politics; The Church; Language and Literature; Personal Names; Effects of the Norman Conquest. All of the kings from Alfred to Eadgar II are dealt with separately and there is a chronicle of events for each of their reigns. There are also maps, family trees and extensive appendices.

£9.95   6 maps & 3 family trees

Looking for the Lost Gods of England
Kathleen Herbert

Kathleen Herbert sifts through the royal genealogies, charms, verse and other sources to find clues to the names and attributes of the Gods and Goddesses of the early English. The earliest account of English heathen practices reveals that they worshipped the Earth Mother and called her Nerthus. The tales, beliefs and traditions of that time are still with us and able to stir our minds and imaginations.

£5.95

Anglo-Saxon Food & Drink
Production, Processing, Distribution, and Consumption
Ann Hagen

Food production for home consumption was the basis of economic activity throughout the Anglo-Saxon period. Used as payment and a medium of trade, food was the basis of the Anglo-Saxons' system of finance and administration.

Information from various sources has been brought together in order to build up a picture of how food was grown, conserved, distributed, prepared and eaten during the period from the beginning of the 5th century to the 11th century. Many people will find it fascinating for the views it gives of an important aspect of Anglo-Saxon life and culture. In addition to Anglo-Saxon England the Celtic west of Britain is also covered.

This edition combines earlier titles – *A Handbook of Anglo-Saxon Food* and *A Second Handbook of Anglo-Saxon Food & Drink*.

Extensive index.

£25   512 pages

Anglo-Saxon Riddles
Translated by John Porter

This is a book full of ingenious characters who speak their names in riddles. Here you will meet a one-eyed garlic seller, a bookworm, an iceberg, an oyster, the sun and moon and a host of others from the everyday life and imagination of the Anglo-Saxons.

John Porter's sparkling translations retain all the vigour and subtly of the original Old English poems, transporting us back over a thousand years to the roots of our language and literature.

Contains all 95 riddles of the Exeter Book in Old English with Modern English translations.

£5.95

The English Elite in 1066 - Gone but not forgotten
Donald Henson

The people listed in this book formed the topmost section of the ruling elite in 1066. It includes all those who held office between the death of Eadward III (January 1066) and the abdication of Eadgar II (December 1066). There are 455 individuals in the main entries and these have been divided according to their office or position.

In addition to the biographical details, there is a wealth of background information about English society and government. A series of appendices provide detailed information about particular topics or groups of people.

£14.95

The Hallowing of England

A guide to the saints of Old England and their places of pilgrimage

Father Andrew Phillips

In the Old English period we can count over 300 saints, yet today their names and exploits are largely unknown. They are part of a forgotten England which, though it lies deep in the past, is an important part of our national and spiritual history.

An alphabetical list of 260 saints cross referenced to an alphabetical list of over 300 places with which the saints are associated; brief biographical details of 22 patriarchs of the English Church; a calendar of saint's feast days.

£5.95

The Battle of Maldon

Text and Translation

Translated and edited by Bill Griffiths

The Battle of Maldon was fought between the men of Essex and the Vikings in AD 991. The action was captured in an Anglo-Saxon poem whose vividness and heroic spirit has fascinated readers and scholars for generations. *The Battle of Maldon* includes the source text; edited text; parallel literal translation; verse translation; notes on pronunciation; review of 103 books and articles. This new edition (the fourth) includes notes on Old English verse.   £5.95

Note: *The Battle of Maldon* and *Beowulf* have been produced with edited Old English texts and parallel literal modern English translations which will be of help to those learning Old English.

Beowulf: Text and Translation

Translated by John Porter

The verse in which the story unfolds is, by common consent, the finest writing surviving in Old English, a text which all students of the language and many general readers will want to tackle in the original form. To aid understanding of the Old English, <u>a literal word-by-word translation</u> is printed opposite the edited text and provides a practical key to this Anglo-Saxon masterpiece. The literal translation is very helpful for those learning or practicing Old English, however, it is not a good way to read the story. For that, we recommend *Beowulf* by Kevin Crossley-Holland – published by Penguin.   £6.95

Remaking the Sutton Hoo Stone

The Ansel-Roper Replica and its Context

Paul Mortimer & Stephen Pollington

The 7th century ship burial at Sutton Hoo contains many enigmatic objects, none more so than the beautifully-worked stone with metal fittings. It is often referred to as a 'sceptre' or 'whetstone' but it may be neither. The techniques used in making the stone and fitments display exceptional craftsmanship. So why were considerable resources devoted to creating it?

The making of a museum quality replica stone has provided new information and fresh insights which may help us answer many of the questions that have been asked about this beautiful and puzzling object.

The techniques used in making the stone are explained as is the geometry embedded within the overall design. There is also a critical review of the existing literature on the subject and a series of essays on aspects of Anglo-Saxon society that may be related to the making of the original stone.

£18.95, 196 pages, Paperback, Illustrations - 106 black & white: 33 colour

The Mead-Hall

The feasting tradition in Anglo-Saxon England
Stephen Pollington

This new study takes a broad look at the subject of halls and feasting in Anglo-Saxon England. The idea of the communal meal was very important among nobles and yeomen, warriors, farmers churchmen and laity. One of the aims of the book is to show that there was not just one 'feast' but two main types: the informal social occasion *gebeorscipe* and the formal, ritual gathering *symbel*.

Using the evidence of Old English texts - mainly the epic *Beowulf* and the *Anglo-Saxon Chronicles*, Stephen Pollington shows that the idea of feasting remained central to early English social traditions long after the physical reality had declined in importance.

The words of the poets and saga-writers are supported by a wealth of archaeological data dealing with halls, settlement layouts and magnificent feasting gear found in many early Anglo-Saxon graves.

Three appendices cover:
- Hall-themes in Old English verse;
- Old English and translated texts;
- The structure and origins of the warband.

£18.95

Tastes of Anglo-Saxon England
Mary Savelli

These easy to follow recipes will enable you to enjoy a mix of ingredients and flavours that were widely known in Anglo-Saxon England but are rarely experienced today. In addition to the 46 recipes, there is background information about households and cooking techniques.

£5.95

Anglo-Saxon Attitudes – A short introduction to Anglo-Saxonism
J.A. Hilton

This is not a book about the Anglo-Saxons, but a book about books about Anglo-Saxons. It describes the academic discipline of Anglo-Saxonism; the methods of study used; the underlying assumptions; and the uses to which it has been put.

Methods and motives have changed over time but right from the start there have been constant themes: English patriotism and English freedom.

£5.95   hardback   64 pages

Tolkien's *Mythology for England* - A Guide to Middle Earth
Edmund Wainwright

You will find here an outline of Tolkien's life and work. The main part of the book consists of an alphabetical subject list which aims to give the reader a greater understanding of Tolkien's Middle-Earth, the creatures that inhabited it and the languages they spoke. The focus is on the Lord of the Rings and how Tolkien's knowledge and enthusiasm for Anglo-Saxon and Norse literature and history helped shape its plot and characters.

£9.95   hardback

The Origins of the Anglo-Saxons
Donald Henson
This book has three great strengths.

First, it pulls together and summarises the whole range of evidence bearing on the subject, offering an up-to-date assessment: the book is, in other words, a highly efficient introduction to the subject. Second – perhaps reflecting Henson's position as a leading practitioner of public archaeology (he is currently Education and Outreach Co-ordinator for the Council for British Archaeology) – the book is refreshingly jargon free and accessible. Third, Henson is not afraid to offer strong, controversial interpretations. The Origins of the Anglo-Saxons can therefore be strongly recommended to those who want a detailed road-map of the evidence and debates for the migration period.
Current Archaeology   £16.95 296 pages

Rudiments of Runelore
Stephen Pollington
The purpose of this book is to provide both a comprehensive introduction for those coming to the subject for the first time, and a handy and inexpensive reference work for those with some knowledge of the subject. The *Abecedarium Nordmannicum* and the English, Norwegian and Icelandic rune poems are included as are two rune riddles, extracts from the Cynewulf poems and new work on the three Brandon runic inscriptions and the Norfolk 'Tiw' runes.

Include: The Origin of the Runes; Runes among the Germans; The Germanic Rune Row and the Common Germanic Language; The English Runic Tradition; The Scandinavian Runic Tradition; Runes and Pseudo-runes; The Use of Runes; Bind Runes and Runic Cryptography.
                                                                      £5.95 Illustrations

Wayland's Work – Anglo-Saxon Art 4th to 7th century
Stephen Pollington
Not only was there considerable artistry in the output of early Anglo-Saxon workshops, but it was vigorous, complex and technically challenging.

The designs found on Anglo-Saxon artefacts are never mere ornament: in a society which used visual and verbal signals to demonstrate power, authority, status and ethnicity, no visual statement was ever empty of meaning.

The aim of this work is to prompt a better understanding of Anglo-Saxon art and the society which produced it. Nothing like this has been published for nearly 100 years.
                                        £49 548 pages 62 colour plates, 226 illustrations

A Departed Music – Readings in Old English Poetry
Walter Nash
The *readings* of this book take the form of passages of translation from some Old English poems. The author paraphrases their content and discuses their place and significance in the history of poetic art in Old English society and culture.

The author's knowledge, enthusiasm and love of his subject help make this an excellent introduction to the subject for students and the general reader.
                                                         £9.95 hardback 240 pages

Organisations

Þa Engliscan Gesiðas

Þa Engliscan Gesiðas (The English Companions) is a historical and cultural society exclusively devoted to Anglo-Saxon history. Its aims are to bridge the gap between scholars and non-experts, and to bring together all those with an interest in the Anglo-Saxon period, its language, culture and traditions. The Fellowship publishes a journal, *Wiðowind*. For further details see www.tha-engliscan-gesithas.org.uk

Regia Anglorum

Our aim is to portray as accurately as possible the life and times of the people who lived in the British Isles around a thousand years ago. We investigate a wide range of crafts and have a Living History Exhibit that frequently erects some thirty tented period structures. We have a large Anglo-Saxon hall and six full scale period boats ranging from 6 metre to 15 metres. www.regia.org   *General information* eolder@regia.org   *Membership* join@regia.org

The Sutton Hoo Society

Our aims and objectives focus on promoting research and education relating to the Anglo-Saxon Royal cemetery at Sutton Hoo, Suffolk in the UK. The Society publishes a newsletter SAXON twice a year. For information about membership see website: www.suttonhoo.org

Wuffing Education

Wuffing Education provides those interested in the history, archaeology, literature and culture of the Anglo-Saxons with the chance to meet experts and fellow enthusiasts for a whole day of in-depth seminars and discussions. Day Schools at Tranmer House, Sutton Hoo, Suffolk. Wuffing Education, 4 Hilly Fields, Woodbridge, Suffolk IP12 4DX, England education@wuffings.co.uk   web www.wuffings.co.uk Tel. 01394 383908 or 01728 688749

Places to visit

Bede's World at Jarrow

Bede's world tells the remarkable story of the life and times of the Venerable Bede. Bede's World, Church Bank, Jarrow, Tyne and Wear, NE32 3DY Tel. 0191 489 2106; Fax: 0191 428 2361; website: www.bedesworld.co.uk

Sutton Hoo near Woodbridge, Suffolk

Sutton Hoo is a group of low burial mounds. Excavations in 1939 brought to light the richest burial ever discovered in Britain. Some original objects as well as replicas of the treasure are on display. National Trust - 2 miles east of Woodbridge on B1083 Tel. 01394 389700

West Stow Anglo-Saxon Village

An early Anglo-Saxon Settlement reconstructed on the site where it was excavated consisting of timber and thatch hall, houses and workshop. There is also a museum containing objects found during the excavation of the site. For details see www.weststow.org or contact: The Visitor Centre, West Stow Country Park, Icklingham Road, West Stow, Bury St Edmunds, Suffolk IP28 6HG Tel. 01284 728718

Lightning Source UK Ltd.
Milton Keynes UK
UKHW050912161020
371634UK00008B/399